Mormonism

Mormonism

by
ANTHONY A. HOEKEMA

WILLIAM B. EERDMANS PUBLISHING COMPANY
Grand Rapids, Michigan

The material in this book is an updating of
material originally appearing in *The Four
Major Cults*, Fourth Printing, August 1972.

Contents

Preface

The discussion of Mormonism found in this book is organized as follows: First, a brief history of Mormonism is given, followed by a description of the organization of the Mormon Church, together with the most recent membership figures. Next the question of the sources of authority appealed to by Mormons is taken up. Then the doctrines taught by the Mormon Church are expounded in the order of the customary divisions of Christian theology: God, man, Christ, salvation, the church, the last things. Finally, an appendix investigates the genuineness of the Book of Mormon.

In setting forth the doctrinal views of the Mormon Church, I have used primary source material exclusively (writings by the original founders of the church and doctrinal works by past and present Mormon leaders). Whenever there was uncertainty about what was being taught on a particular doctrinal point, information was obtained directly from Mormon headquarters. References to the source materials used are given in the footnotes; a bibliography lists additional primary and secondary sources. All Scripture quotations not otherwise identified are from the American Standard Version.

Readers of this book are referred to the author's *Four Major Cults* (Eerdmans, 1963) for additional material on the cults. Besides dealing with the doctrinal teachings of Christian Science, Jehovah's Witnesses, and Seventh-day Adventism, *The Four Major Cults* also includes chapters on the challenge of the cults, the distinctive traits of the cult, and the approach to the cultist.

May the Lord use this book for the advancement of His kingdom and for the glory of His name. May He particularly use it to lead many from the errors of Mormonism to the truth as it is in Christ.

Anthony A. Hoekema

Grand Rapids, Michigan
July, 1972

I. History

THERE IS PROBABLY NO AMERICAN RELIGIOUS GROUP WHICH HAS had a more colorful or fascinating history than the Mormons. The Mormon trek to Salt Lake City in 1846-47, for example, has become an integral part of the American saga of the settlement of the West. I shall reproduce here only as much of this history as will enable us to place Mormonism into its proper setting, and will serve to acquaint us with its outstanding leaders.[1]

JOSEPH SMITH

Joseph Smith, Jr., was born on December 23, 1805, in Sharon, Vermont, the third son of Joseph and Lucy Smith. In 1817, when Joseph was 11, the family settled near Palmyra, New York, not far from present-day Rochester. A few years later most of the members of the family had joined the Presbyterian church, but Joseph was undecided as to which church he should join. There was so much strife among the denominations, he felt, that he could not decide who was right and who was wrong.

In describing the following events, I am drawing upon Smith's own autobiography as reproduced in one of the sacred books of Mormonism, *Pearl of Great Price,* under the heading, "Extracts from the History of Joseph Smith, the Prophet" (pp. 46-57). While puzzling about which church to join, so Smith tells us, he read James 1:5, "If any of you lack wisdom, let him ask of God, that giveth to all men liberally, and upbraideth not; and it shall be

---

[1] Readers desiring more complete treatments of Mormon history are referred to the biographical and historical titles listed in the bibliography.

given him.["](2) Accordingly, he continues, I retired to the woods, knelt down, and began to pray. Suddenly two "Personages" appeared. One of them pointed to the other and said, "This is my Beloved Son. Hear Him!" In answer to the question as to which of the "sects" was right, the one Personage who had addressed me, so Smith goes on, said that I was to join none of them, since "they were all wrong," and since "all their creeds were an abomination in his sight" — that, in fact, those professing their faith in these various "sects" were all corrupt and hypocritical.[3] This vision, Smith alleges, occurred in the early spring of 1820. It will be observed that Smith would then have been only 14 years old.

On September 21, 1823, Smith continues, I had a second vision. A personage appeared at my bedside who was glorious beyond description. He said that he was a messenger sent from the presence of God, and that his name was Moroni; that God had a work for me to do, and that "my name should be had for good and evil among all nations, kindreds and tongues." He told me that a book had been deposited, written on golden plates, giving an account of the former inhabitants of this continent and containing "the fulness of the everlasting Gospel" as delivered by the Saviour to the ancient inhabitants of this land. He also said that there were "two stones in silver bows — and these stones, fastened to a breastplate, constituted what is called the Urim and Thummim — deposited with the plates," adding that God had prepared these stones for the purpose of translating this book.[4]

In the vision, Smith says, I was shown exactly where the plates

---

[2] Joseph Smith, *The Pearl of Great Price* (Salt Lake City: Church of Jesus Christ of Latter-Day Saints, 1952), p. 47.

[3] *Ibid.,* p. 48.

[4] *Ibid.,* pp. 50, 51. It will be observed that in the Bible the Urim and Thummim are mentioned as means whereby the will of the Lord was ascertained in certain judicial matters (Num. 27:21, I Sam. 28:6, I Sam. 14:41 in RSV). No reference is ever made in the Old Testament to their use as an aid in translating documents. In Smith's vision, however, the Urim and Thummim were stones affixed to silver bows so as to look like a pair of spectacles. From p. 55 of *The Pearl of Great Price* we learn that the Urim and Thummim were used by Smith as means whereby he translated the characters on the golden plates (cf. Mormon 9:34 in the *Book of Mormon*; also *Doctrine and Covenants* [Salt Lake City, 1952], sections 8 and 9). It is thus obvious that Joseph Smith's understanding of the use of the Urim and Thummim was quite different from that of the Old Testament writers. It is also important to note that, according to Smith's own admission, the characters on the golden plates could not be translated without the aid of the Urim and Thummim.

had been deposited. That same night the heavenly messenger appeared again twice, each time repeating the same message.[5]

The next day, Smith continues, I went to a hill outside the vil-
lage where we lived (called the hill Cumorah) and found the
golden plates deposited in a stone box with the Urim and Thummim and the breastplate. I was not permitted to take them out
at this time, however, but was told by the angel, who had re-
appeared, that I should come back to this place every year at this
time for the next four years.[6] Finally, however, on September 22,
1827, I was given the plates by the heavenly messenger, with in-
structions to keep them carefully until he, the angel, should call for
them again.[7]

It should be mentioned here that some months previous to this
date, on January 18, 1827, Smith had been married to Emma
Hale, of Harmony, Pennsylvania, having eloped with her after
Emma's father had refused to give his consent to their marriage.
The "official" reason for this refusal, according to Smith's autobiography, was the persecution which attended Smith because of
the vision he claimed to have seen.[8] Fawn M. Brodie, however,
in her biography of Joseph Smith, gives documentary evidence to
prove that the real reason for Mr. Hale's refusal was that at this
time Smith's only occupation was that of digging for money with
the help of a "peepstone" into which he would gaze to determine
the location of the treasure.[9]

Smith goes on to tell us that because of the persecution which
followed his reception of the plates he decided to move to the
house of his wife's father in Harmony, Pennsylvania. There he
began to copy the characters off the plates and, by means of the
Urim and Thummim, to translate some of them.

At about this time Mr. Martin Harris, a New York farmer who
was befriending Smith and was planning to finance the publication of the book which would result from the translation of the
plates, wanted to have some assurance that the plates were genuine and that they were being translated correctly. Though Harris
was first under the impression that the characters on the golden
plates were Hebrew, Smith explained to him that they were actu-

5 *Pearl of Great Price*, p. 52.
6 *Ibid.*, p. 53.
7 *Ibid.*, p. 54.
8 *Ibid.*, p. 54.
9 *No Man Knows My History* (New York: Knopf, 1957), pp. 29-33;
see also her Appendix A, pp. 405-18.

ally an altered or "Reformed" Egyptian.[10] To satisfy Harris, Smith gave him the characters that had been copied from the plates; Harris then took these characters, together with a translation of them, to a certain Professor Charles Anthon in New York City. According to Smith's autobiography, Professor Anthon identified the characters supposedly copied from the plates as "Egyptian, Chaldaic, Assyriac, and Arabic," and affirmed that the translation of them was correct, "more so than any he had before seen translated from the Egyptian."[11]

In April of 1829, Smith continues, a former schoolteacher, Oliver Cowdery, joined me. I now commenced to translate the *Book of Mormon,* and he began to copy down what I told him to write. In May of 1829 we went into the woods to pray. While we were praying, a heavenly messenger, who identified himself as John the Baptist, descended and conferred upon both Oliver and myself the priesthood of Aaron. Both of us now began to prophesy and to understand the true meaning of the Scriptures.[12]

Shortly after this, so it is claimed, the Melchizedek, or higher, priesthood was also conferred upon Joseph Smith and Oliver Cowdery at a place along the banks of the Susquehanna River, by Peter, James, and John.[13]

On one of the opening pages of every copy of the *Book of Mormon,* the reader will find the so-called *Testimony of Three Witnesses.* Smith had been told that he was not to show the plates to anyone except to certain witnesses who were to be designated by divine revelation.[14] Joseph Fielding Smith tells the story of these three witnesses. After the translation of the *Book of Mormon* had been completed, the following three men desired to be the witnesses of the golden plates: Oliver Cowdery, David Whitmer, and Martin Harris. These three men went out into the

---

[10] Cf. Mormon 9:32, 33.

[11] *Pearl of Great Price,* p. 55. It should be observed that to combine Arabic script and Egyptian characters (whether hieroglyphic, hieratic, or demotic) would be a linguistic monstrosity. Further, note the letter from Charles Anthon to E. D. Howe, reproduced by Walter Martin, in which Anthon asserts, "The whole story about my having pronounced the Mormonite inscription to be 'reformed Egyptian hieroglyphics' is perfectly false." *The Maze of Mormonism* (Grand Rapids: Zondervan, 1962), p. 42.

[12] *Pearl of Great Price,* pp. 56-57.

[13] Joseph Fielding Smith, *Essentials in Church History* (Salt Lake City: Deseret News Press, 1953), p. 69. Mr. Smith was the official church historian of the Mormon Church.

[14] See Ether 5:2-4, II Nephi 27:12-13, and cf. *Doctrine and Covenants* 5:11ff.

woods with Smith and knelt in prayer. Suddenly an angel stood before them, holding the plates in his hands and turning them leaf by leaf.[15]

Apparently not satisfied with the witness of these three men, Smith later called eight other witnesses to view the plates and to give their testimony — a testimony which one will also find in every authentic copy of the *Book of Mormon*.[16]

On March 26, 1830, the *Book of Mormon,* now complete, was first placed on sale in the Palmyra bookstore. The first printing was financed by Martin Harris, who had had to mortgage his farm to pay for it.

On April 6, 1830, at Fayette, New York, the "Church of Jesus Christ of Latter-day Saints" was officially organized; that same year the church was incorporated. There were but six members at first, the oldest being only thirty-one years of age. Smith and Cowdery ordained each other as elders. Within a month the number of members had jumped to forty.

Since the *Book of Mormon* contained the story of the ancestry of the American Indians, it was but natural that the early Mor-

---

[15] J. F. Smith, *op. cit.,* pp. 72-77 (cf. *Doctrine and Covenants,* Section 17). Robert F. Boyd, in "Mormonism," *Interpretation,* X, No. 4 (Oct., 1956), informs us that two of these men, Whitmer and Cowdery, were later charged by their fellow Mormons as thieves and counterfeiters, and that the other witness, Martin Harris, later changed his solemn testimony to the following statement: "Why, I did not see them as I do that pencil case, yet I saw them with the eye of faith. I saw them just as distinctly as I saw anything about me — though at the time they were covered over with a cloth" (p. 431; see Brodie, *op. cit.,* p. 78; and cf. James H. Snowden, *The Truth About Mormonism* [New York, 1926], pp. 71ff.). All three of these witnesses later became apostates from the Mormon Church, though two of them, Cowdery and Harris, were eventually rebaptized (Brodie, p. 78; see *Essentials in Church History,* pp. 208-209, and note b). The question cannot be suppressed: how much weight is to be attached to a testimony coming from men of this sort?

[16] J. F. Smith, *op. cit.,* pp. 77-78. It is significant to note that four of these eight witnesses were Whitmers, relatives of the David Whitmer who had signed the first testimony; that Hiram Page, a fifth, had married a Whitmer daughter; and that the other three were members of "the prophet's" own family: his father and his brothers Hyrum and Samuel. One is not impressed with the impartiality of this group. Three of these eight witnesses later left the Mormon Church (*ibid.,* p. 209, note b). Further, it is to be remembered that the "divine revelations" alluded to in n. 14, above, had only specified that there were to be three witnesses who were to see the plates. One wonders by what authority Smith now obtained the testimony of these eight additional witnesses. Did he, perhaps, have some doubts as to the reliability of the first three?

mons should feel a sense of mission to the Indians.[17]   Accordingly, a number of Mormons now went to Kirtland, Ohio (not far from present-day Cleveland, on the Lake Erie shore); here the Mormon gospel was preached and a number of converts were baptized.   Later a temple was built at Kirtland.   New revelations were now coming to "the prophet" on many subjects.   While the group was at Kirtland, Smith compiled and published the first edition of a second Mormon sacred book, *Doctrine and Covenants.* Not satisfied with the Bible, Smith also at this time worked on a revision of the King James Version of the Scriptures.

Mormons had already begun moving farther west, to Jackson County, Missouri, where the city of Independence was located. Smith now received a revelation telling him that Jackson County, Missouri, was "the land of promise, and the place for the city of Zion."[18]   Hence many of Smith's followers now began to settle in Independence, Missouri.   The non-Mormon residents of Independence, however, did not take kindly to the claim that God had chosen this land for the Mormons.   Mobs began to attack the Mormons; consequently they went north and founded the town of Far West, Missouri.

Here, too, however, troubles continued.   After a number of battles had been fought between the settlers and the Mormons, the state militia intervened.   Smith and other Mormon leaders were imprisoned.   Eventually, however, the Mormons all escaped and joined the other "saints," who had by this time moved east to Illinois.   Here, in 1839, Joseph Smith chose a site on the Mississippi River, about fifty miles above Quincy, as their new home.   He called it Nauvoo (which, he asserted, was Hebrew for "beautiful place").   At this time Smith organized the so-called Nauvoo Legion, a small standing army, permitting himself to be called its lieutenant- general.   Here, in Nauvoo, the construction of another Mormon temple was begun, and intense missionary activity continued.

Trouble began for Smith, however, when the *Nauvoo Expositor,* an anti-Mormon paper, began to publish material which was unfavorable to the Mormons.   Smith therefore ordered his men to destroy the *Expositor's* press and to burn every copy of the paper that could be found.   When the owners of the press complained to

[17] Charles S. Braden, *These Also Believe* (New York: Macmillan, 1960), p. 427.

[18] *Doctrine and Covenants,* 57:1-2.

the governor of the state about this wanton destruction of their property, Smith was arrested.   He was released, but later re-arrested, together with his brother Hyrum, and was taken to the city jail in Carthage, Illinois, a few miles from Nauvoo.   On June 27, 1844, a mob attacked the jail and killed both Joseph and Hyrum Smith. The opponents of Mormonism thus hurt their cause, since Smith now became in Mormon eyes a martyred hero.

BRIGHAM YOUNG

After Smith's death, the burning question of the day was: who would become the new Mormon leader? Very little thought had been given to the subject of succession in the presidency since it had been assumed that Smith still had many years to live. Sidney Rigdon, who had become a member of the church in Kirtland, Ohio, and had worked in close association with Joseph Smith since that time, first presented his claim to be the new "guardian" of the church, basing his claim on the fact that he had been named the first counselor to President Smith.   At a later meeting, how-ever, Brigham Young claimed that the authority of the presidency now rested with the twelve apostles, of which group he was the president.   The Mormons accepted his leadership, and thus Young (1801-1877) became the second president of the Mormon church.[19]

Having been notified by the State of Illinois that they had to leave Nauvoo, the Mormons, under the leadership of Brigham Young, made plans to move to the west.   One of the Mormons described their journey from Nauvoo to the west as "four hundred wagons moving to — we know not where."   In early February of 1846 the epic journey to the west began. There were many hard-ships along the way: cold, exposure, storms, Indians, quarrels, apostasy, inadequate food and clothing.   On July 24, 1847, the caravan arrived at the Salt Lake Valley in Utah; when President Young first saw the valley, he expressed his satisfaction in the memorable words, "This is the place!"   He then proceeded to lo-cate the site of the proposed new city (since known as Salt Lake City) about ten miles east of the lake.

Salt Lake City has been the headquarters of the Mormon Church ever since.   Between 1856 and 1860 some 3,000 converts pushed handcarts from Iowa City, then the end of the railroad, to the Salt

19 Joseph Fielding Smith, *op. cit.,* pp. 385-89.

Lake Valley — a distance of about 1300 miles. Through Young's leadership a revolving fund was set up to finance immigration from foreign countries, particularly Great Britain and the Scandinavian countries. In 1877, when Brigham Young died, there were 140,000 Mormons.[20]

THE MORMON CHURCH

The Church of Jesus Christ of Latter-Day Saints is today divided into approximately 562 stakes, 4342 wards, and 793 independent branches. A stake is a larger grouping of churches comparable to a diocese, presbytery, or classis; the average number of members in a stake is about 4,000, though this number may vary widely. A ward is comparable to a local organized church; the average number of members in a ward is approximately 600, though it may run as high as 1200. An independent branch is a "ward in embryo," comparable to a new church not yet organized; the membership of an independent branch usually runs from 50 to about 200 persons. In addition to the groupings just named, there are at present 1,942 mission branches and 98 full-time missions.[21]

According to the statistical report of the Mormon Church published at the time of the General Conference in April, 1972, and giving figures as of December 31, 1971, the world membership of the Mormon Church on that date was 3,090,953, representing an increase of 94 percent since 1960.[22] Of this number 2,133,072 were found in the United States, and 957,881 were to be found outside the United States.[23] As of December, 1971, therefore, the foreign membership of the Mormon Church is approximately one-third of the total membership; thus about two out of every three Mormons in the world are to be found in the United States.

In the United States, the greatest number of Mormons are to be found in Utah, but there are members of the church in virtually every state of the union. Outside of the United States, Mormons are most numerous in South America, the Pacific Islands, Mexico, Great Britain, Germany, Scandinavia, and Canada, although there is a

[20] Hartzell Spence, "The Mormon Church," *Reader's Digest,* April, 1958, p. 190.

[21] The above information was obtained from the following sources: a letter from Spencer W. Kimball of the Council of the Twelve Apostles, dated April 16, 1963; and a Church Statistical Report published in April, 1972, giving figures as of December 31, 1971.

[22] According to this report, 83,514 converts were baptized in stakes and missions in 1971, and there was a net increase during 1971 of 160,143 members.

[23] From a letter to the author from Mark E. Petersen of the Council of Twelve Apostles dated June 26, 1972.

considerable membership in Asia and Central America.[24] Mormons have fifteen temples now in operation: six in Utah (at Salt Lake City, Logan, Manti, Ogden, Provo, and St. George); two in California (in Los Angeles and Oakland); one in Mesa, Arizona; one in Idaho Falls, Idaho; one in Laie, Hawaii; one in Cardston in the Canadian province of Alberta; and one each in England, Switzerland, and New Zealand. Another temple now being constructed in Washington, D.C., is expected to be in operation within the next two years. In these temples, which may be entered only by Mormons in good standing, two types of ceremonies, very important in present-day Mormonism, are performed: celestial marriage and baptism for the dead. The best-known Mormon temple is the one at Salt Lake City, built between the years 1853 and 1893 and located on Temple Square. The other prominent building on Temple Square is the Tabernacle, open to the public, from which the world-famous Tabernacle Choir broadcasts every Sunday morning.

Mormons recognize two orders of priesthood: the lesser, called the Aaronic priesthood, and the greater, known as the Melchizedek priesthood. Every male Mormon may belong to one or the other of these two priesthoods, provided that his understanding of the teachings of the church and his daily life are in conformity with church requirements. One must, however, be at least twelve years old to be eligible for the Aaronic priesthood and at least nineteen to be eligible for the Melchizedek priesthood. The office-bearers with the highest authority must be members of the Melchizedek priesthood. The highest governing body of the church is the so-called First Presidency, consisting of the President of the Church and two Counselors to the President. The current President of the Mormon Church is Harold B. Lee. Next in the line of authority is the Council of Twelve Apostles.

> They [the Council of Twelve] constitute a quorum whose unanimous decisions are equally binding in power and authority with those of the First Presidency of the Church. When the First Presidency is disorganized through the death or disability of the President, the directing authority in government reverts at once to the Quorum of the Twelve Apostles, by whom the nomination to the Presidency is made.[25]

[24] This information was obtained from the July 1, 1972, issue of *Church News*, an official publication of the Church of Jesus Christ of Latter-day Saints. The first-named (South America) has the most Mormons outside the United States, the second the second largest number, and so on.
[25] James E. Talmage, *Articles of Faith* (Salt Lake City: Church of Jesus Christ of Latter-day Saints, 1957), p. 210.

It is a well-known fact that many Mormons dedicate two years of their lives to missionary service. According to an authoritative Mormon source, there are currently about 14,000 Mormon missionaries in the field. These include a few older couples and a sprinkling of young women. Most of these, however, are young men. About one-third of Mormon young men between the ages of 19 and 25 go on these missions. Less than 5 percent of the girls go out; they are not encouraged to go, since missionary work is deemed to be primarily the work of men holding the priesthood. All of these missionaries (or their parents or close friends) pay their own expenses. The Mormon Church does not support any missionaries. This work is entirely a free-will offering on the part of those who go out.[25a]

It is of interest to note that tithing is mandatory for Mormons (see *Doctrine and Covenants* 119 and 120). In accordance with the so-called "Word of Wisdom" found in *Doctrines and Covenants* 89, Mormons are not permitted to use tobacco, to drink liquor in any form, or to drink tea or coffee.

Elmer T. Clark, in his *Small Sects in America*, lists five groups that have split off from the Mormons. Of these the largest is the Reorganized Church of Jesus Christ of Latter Day Saints, which has its headquarters in Independence, Missouri. This body, which broke away from the other Mormons when the followers of Brigham Young moved to Salt Lake City, claims to be the real and legal successor of the church founded by Joseph Smith. According to Cecil R. Ettinger of the Council of Twelve Apostles of the Reorganized Church, the world membership of this body as of June 30, 1971, was 203,406, of which 164,465 were to be found in the United States and Canada.[25b]

[25a] The information given in the above paragraph is based on two letters to the author from Mark E. Petersen of the Council of Twelve, one dated July 6, 1962, and the other August 11, 1971.
[25b] Letter from Cecil R. Ettinger dated August 10, 1971.

II. Source of Authority

The Pearl of Great Price, one of the Mormon sacred books, contains a series of statements written by Joseph Smith, entitled "The Articles of Faith" (p. 59). These articles are still authoritative for the Mormon Church today. In fact, they form the basis for one of the best-known Mormon doctrinal works: *A Study of the Articles of Faith,* by James E. Talmage. Article 8 of these Articles of Faith reads as follows: "We believe the Bible to be the word of God as far as it is translated correctly; we also believe the Book of Mormon to be the word of God."

Mormons, therefore, have many reservations as to the correctness of past and present Bible translations. It is to be observed, however, that they do not make a similar reservation with regard to the *Book of Mormon,* since they contend that Joseph Smith was the inspired translator of the latter. The following quotation from James E. Talmage, one of the most authoritative writers on Mormon doctrines, will bear out this point:

> It is noticeable that we make no reservation respecting the Book of Mormon on the ground of incorrect translation. To do so would be to ignore attested facts as to the bringing forth of that book. Joseph Smith the prophet, seer, and revelator, through whom the ancient record has been translated into our modern tongue, expressly avers that the translation was effected through the gift and power of God, and is in no sense the product of linguistic scholarship.[26]

We may note that here already we have a point at which Mor-

26 *The Vitality of Mormonism* (Boston: Gorham Press, 1919), p. 127.

mons consider the *Book of Mormon* to be superior to the Bible: there are said to be errors of translation in the Bible, whereas no such errors are said to exist in the *Book of Mormon*.[27]

BIBLE VERSION

We consider next the question of the version of the Bible used by the Mormon Church. Before we can discuss this question, however, we must remind ourselves of the previously mentioned fact that, while the Mormons were in Kirtland, Ohio, Joseph Smith worked on a revision of the King James version of the Bible. What was the nature of this revision? On the basis of Article 8 of the Articles of Faith, one would assume that this revision of the Bible would involve nothing more than possible improvements in the English translation. As a matter of fact, this is the impression given by Mormon author John A. Widtsoe: "The prophet Joseph Smith, from the beginning of his ministry, gave some time to revising passages in the Bible which had been translated incorrectly or so rendered as to make the meaning obscure."[28]

This impression, however, is quite contrary to fact. What Smith did when he revised the Bible was not at all merely a matter of improving the translation, as we shall see. Neither did Smith's work bear the slightest resemblance to textual criticism, in which Widtsoe also affirms that he was engaged.[29] Textual critics carefully compare one Bible manuscript with another in the attempt to establish which of various readings of a given passage was the original one. What Smith did, however, had nothing whatever to do with manuscript study of this sort; it was rather a complete rewriting of certain Bible passages in the light of supposed new revelations.

The Reorganized Church of Jesus Christ of Latter Day Saints, a group which severed relations with the main Mormon body in 1844 and was organized as a separate body in 1853, has pub-

---

[27] This is a strange claim, indeed, in view of the fact that some 3,000 changes have been made in the text of the *Book of Mormon* since the publication of the first edition! For a more extended discussion of this point, see the Appendix.

[28] *Evidences and Reconciliations,* arranged by G. Homer Durham (Salt Lake City: Bookcraft, 1960), p. 117.

[29] *Ibid.,* p. 118.

lished Joseph Smith's revision of the King James Bible.[30]   Even
a casual perusal of this volume will reveal that Smith made a
great many changes in the Bible text which went far beyond
mere "translation" corrections.   One notices these changes already in the opening chapters of Genesis.   These chapters are
recast as a direct revelation to Moses in which God speaks in the
first person: "And I, God, said, Let there be light, and there was
light" (Gen. 1:6, Inspired Version).   Completely new material
is inserted into Genesis 3: the story of Satan's coming before
God and offering to be sent into the world to redeem mankind,
if only he can receive God's honor. When this offer is refused
by God, Satan rebels against God (Gen. 3:1-5, Inspired Version).
An entirely new section is added which describes Adam's baptism
by immersion (Gen. 6:67, Inspired Version).   A long new section is added, giving the prophecy of Enoch (Gen. 6:26-7:78, Inspired Version), and telling that not only Enoch but an entire
group of saints, the people of Zion, were taken up into heaven.
Furthermore, in these early chapters of Genesis such distinctive
Mormon doctrines are revealed as the pre-existence of the souls
of all men (Gen. 2:6, 9, Inspired Version); the teaching that
if man had not sinned he would not have been able to propagate
himself (Gen. 6:56, Inspired Version); the teaching that the
children of Canaan were made black as a curse for their sins
(Gen. 7:10, Inspired Version); and the teaching that the earth
shall have rest for a thousand years after the Lord returns (Gen.
7:72, Inspired Version).[31]

Smith revised many more sections of the Bible, both in the
Old Testament and in the New.[32]   One of the most significant

[30] INSPIRED VERSION: *The Holy Scriptures, Containing the Old and New
Testaments*: An Inspired Revision of the Authorized Version, by Joseph
Smith, Junior.   A New Corrected Edition. Independence, Mo.: Herald
Pub. House, 1955 (originally published in 1867). The reason why this
version was published by the Reorganized Church is as follows: the original manuscript of this revision was in the possession of Emma Smith,
widow of Joseph Smith, Jr.   She refused to follow Brigham Young's leadership, and also refused to turn over this manuscript to the main Mormon
body.   Mormons claim, however, that a copy of this revision, made by
John M. Bernhisel, is in the possession of the Utah Church (Joseph Fielding Smith, *Answers to Gospel Questions* [Salt Lake City; Deseret Book Co.,
1958], II, 206).
[31] It is revealing to note that in this supposedly superior bit of divine revelation such grammatical errors occur as "for as I, the Lord God, liveth"
(Gen. 3:30), and "surely the flocks of my brother falleth into my hands"
(Gen. 5:18).
[32] For further details, see George B. Arbaugh, *Revelation in Mormonism*
(Chicago: University of Chicago Press, 1932), Chap. 8.

additions was the insertion into Genesis 50 of a passage in which his own future appearance was predicted: "And that seer will I bless . . . and his name shall be called Joseph, and it shall be after the name of his father . . . for the thing which the Lord shall bring forth by his hand shall bring my people unto salvation."[33]

It is quite evident, therefore, that what Smith did when he revised the Bible was something far more drastic than merely correcting its translation. The question must therefore now be asked: which version of the Bible do Mormons accept? As we have seen, the Reorganized Church, the largest of the Mormon splinter groups, uses Smith's Inspired Version as its official text. The Mormon Church,[34] however, does not use the Inspired Version; its official Bible version is the King James. Authorities in the Mormon Church, however, make it very clear that they do accept the changes made in the King James Version by Joseph Smith. Note what Joseph Fielding Smith, currently President of the Council of Twelve Apostles, has to say about this:

> The reason why the Church of Jesus Christ of Latter-Day Saints has not published the entire manuscript [of the Inspired Version of the Bible] is not due to any lack of confidence in the integrity of Joseph Smith, or doubt as to the correctness of the numerous additions and changes which are not in the Authorized Version of the Bible. The members of the Church do accept fully all of these and additions as having come by divine revelations to the Prophet Joseph Smith.[35]

Compare also the following statement by the same author:

> The revision of the Bible which was done by Joseph Smith at the command of the Lord was not a complete revision of the Bible. There are many parts of the Bible in which the Prophet did not change the meaning where it is incorrect. . . . However, all that he did is very helpful for the major errors have been corrected.[36]

Why, then, has not the Mormon Church, like the Reorganized

---

[33] Gen. 50:33, Inspired Version. Cf. II Nephi 3:15.

[34] The expression, "the Mormon Church," shall always be used to designate the Salt Lake City Mormons; whenever the word "Mormon" is used without further qualification, it refers to this group. The expression "Reorganized Church" will be used for the group which has its headquarters in Independence, Missouri.

[35] *Answers to Gospel Questions,* II, 207.

[36] *Doctrines of Salvation* (Salt Lake City: Bookcraft, 1956), III, 191.

Church, adopted Smith's Inspired Version as its official Bible?
Mormons give at least two reasons for this:

(1) The Inspired Version has not been published by the
Mormon Church because it was never completed. Smith, it is
alleged, wished to complete the revision, but was prevented
from doing so by persecution and mob violence.[37] This is,
however, rather strange reasoning. If certain errors in the Bible
have been corrected by Smith, as is alleged, why continue to use
an erroneous version? Why not use as many of the "corrections"
as there are?

(2) The Inspired Version is not used by the Mormon Church
because there are such differences between this version and the
versions in common use that the employment of the former
would be a hindrance in mission work. The King James Version
is therefore said to "give us a common ground for proselyting
purposes."[38] This answer is also hard to understand. Do the
missionaries then intend to deceive people as to which Bible
they accept? Furthermore, why not eliminate the *Book of Mormon,* then, since this would, on the ground mentioned above,
constitute an even greater hindrance? Besides, even if missionaries should go out with a King James Version, why should
not the church publish the Inspired Version for use by Mormons
only?

(3) A third reason may be added: an important section of the
Inspired Version, the so-called Book of Moses (which is an
exact copy of the opening chapters of Genesis in the Inspired
Version, containing the additional material referred to above),
has been incorporated into the Mormon sacred book, *Pearl of
Great Price.* This part of Smith's revised Bible, therefore, the
Mormons do retain — though alongside of the King James version
of these chapters, which is quite different, as we have seen.

We conclude from this discussion that the statement made
in Article 8 of the Articles of Faith is not honest and not true:
"We believe the Bible to be the word of God as far as it is
translated correctly. . . ." Mormons believe no such thing.
They hold that the Bible as we have it is not correct on a number
of significant points and that some serious omissions are found
in it. They do not therefore consider the Bible as such to be
either complete or authoritative in its unemended form. More

[37] Joseph Fielding Smith, *Answers to Gospel Questions,* II, 207.
[38] *Ibid.*

honest than Article 8 is the following statement by Mormon
author Bruce R. McConkie:

> The Book of Moses, a work containing eight chapters and
> covering the same general period and events as are found in the
> first six chapters of Genesis, contains much of this restored
> truth.   The 1st and 7th chapters of Moses are entirely new
> revelations having no counterpart in Genesis.   The other
> chapters in Moses cover the same events recorded in the first
> six chapters of Genesis, but the account revealed in latter-days
> has been so enlarged, contains so much new material, and so
> radically changes the whole perspective of the Lord's dealings
> with Adam and the early patriarchs that for all practical purposes
> it may be considered as entirely new matter.   The whole view
> of. the creation of all things; of pre-existence and the purpose
> of life; of Adam and his fall; of the primeval revelation of the
> gospel to man; of the terms and conditions in accordance with
> which salvation is offered to the living and the dead; of Enoch,
> his ministry and his establishment of Zion; and of Noah, his
> priesthood and ministry — the whole view and perspective
> relative to all these things is radically changed by the new
> revelations in the Book of Moses.   This book, which is also
> contained in the Prophet's Inspired Version of the Bible, is
> one of the most important documents the Lord has ever re-
> vealed.[39]

Honest and forthright is also the following quotation from Joseph
Fielding Smith: "Guided by the *Book of Mormon, Doctrine and
Covenants,* and the Spirit of the Lord, it is not difficult for one
to discern the errors in the Bible."[40]

We may thus note a second respect in which Mormons consider their sacred books to be superior to the Bible: the Bible as
it stands is not only full of errors but is in dire need of supple-
mentary material and revised readings, which have been supplied,
at least in part, by Joseph Smith.

At this point the reader is referred to Jesus' Parable of
the Rich man and Lazarus, found in Luke 16:19-31. It will be
recalled that the rich man, after he lifted up his eyes and found
himself in Hades, asked that his brothers be given an additional
revelation besides what was in the Bible: namely, that Lazarus
be sent to them from the realm of the dead. Abraham, however,
replied: "If they hear not Moses and the prophets, neither will

[39] *Mormon Doctrine* (Salt Lake City: Bookcraft, 1958), pp. 509-10.
[40] *Doctrines of Salvation,* III, 191.

they be persuaded, if one rise from the dead" (v. 31). Here Christ clearly disavowed the need for a source of revelation additional to the Bible. The "Moses and the prophets" of which Jesus spoke, furthermore, were not Joseph Smith's emended version, but the Old Testament as we have it. Apparently the Mormons wish to be wiser than Christ Himself.

More needs to be said on this point, however. Mormons arrogate to Joseph Smith an authority which was not claimed even by Jesus Christ: namely, the authority to alter the text of Scripture! When Christ confronted Satan in the wilderness, He answered the tempter by quoting three passages from the Book of Deuteronomy, prefixing these quotations with the words, "It is written" (Mt. 4:4, 7, 10). By these prefixed words our Lord indicated the finality and unchangeability of the words of Scripture. Christ further affirmed the inviolability of the law (which word here probably stands for the entire Old Testament) in Luke 16:17, "But it is easier for heaven and earth to pass away, than for one tittle of the law to fall." Christ emphatically asserted the inviolability of the Scriptures in John 10:35, "The scripture cannot be broken. . . ." Never did our Lord take it upon Himself to alter one word of the Old Testament Scriptures, nor did He ever suggest that a time was coming when certain Old Testament passages would be altered through further revelation. Yet Joseph Smith dared to assume authority which Christ never claimed — dared to tamper with the Word of God. The reader may judge for himself what this fact tells us about the attitude of the Mormon Church toward the Bible.

We have already observed in the preceding paragraphs that the Bible as it stands is not sufficient for the Mormons. In addition to emending and revising the text of the Scriptures, however, Mormons have added to them three additional sacred books: *The Book of Mormon, Doctrine and Covenants,* and *The Pearl of Great Price.* Let us examine each of these in turn.

THE BOOK OF MORMON

The Book of Mormon, it will be recalled, was referred to in Article 8 of the Articles of Faith: "We also believe the Book of Mormon to be the word of God." This book takes pains to assert its own *raison d'être.* In I Nephi 13:28 an angel is said to have revealed to Nephi that "after the book [the Bible] hath gone forth through the hands of the great and abominable church,[41] . . . there are many plain and precious things taken away from the book. . ." We have already seen that Smith attempted to supply some of these "plain and precious things" by revising the Bible. However, Mormons teach that an entirely new book was necessary to complete God's revelation to man. This point is made clear in a section of the *Book of Mormon* where God is quoted as saying through Nephi:

> Thou fool, that shall say: A Bible, we have got a Bible, and we need no more Bible. . . . And because that I have spoken one word ye need not suppose that I cannot speak another. . . . Wherefore, because that ye have a Bible ye need not suppose that it contains all my words; neither need ye suppose that I have not caused more to be written.[42]

Bruce McConkie, therefore, is only echoing the *Book of Mormon* when he makes the startling statement: "One of the great heresies of an apostate Christianity is the unfounded assumption that the Bible contains all of the inspired teachings now extant among men."[43]

What is the *Book of Mormon* all about? Briefly, it is an account of two great waves of immigration to the American continents. The first of these, described only in the Book of Ether, was that of the nation of the Jaredites. They left from the region around the Tower of Babel at about 2,250 B.C. Jared's brother, a prophet, was told by the Lord to build eight barges for the ocean trip. These barges were supposed to be as long as a tree, and were to be made "exceeding tight, even that they would hold water like unto a dish" (Ether 2:17). When Jared's brother informed the Lord that there would not be sufficient air in the barges to allow the occupants to breathe, the Lord said to him,

> Behold, thou shalt make a hole in the top, and also in the bottom; and when thou shalt suffer for air thou shalt unstop the hole and receive air. And if it be so that the water come in upon thee, behold, ye shall stop the hole, that ye may not perish in the flood (Ether 2:20).

[41] Presumably the Roman Catholic Church — see Bruce McConkie, *Mormon Doctrine*, p. 130.
[42] II Nephi 29:6, 9, and 10.
[43] *Op. cit.*, p. 79.

These eight barges, driven by the wind for three hundred forty-four days, landed at exactly the same time and at exactly the same place: the West Coast of Central America. Here, in America, the Jaredites founded a widespread civilization and built many cities; we are particularly informed that "they also had horses, and asses, and there were elephants and cureloms and cumoms; all of which were useful unto man, and more especially the elephants and cureloms and cumoms" (Ether 9:19). The Jaredites, however, did not get along well with each other; they engaged in savage battles, in one of which two million mighty men, plus their wives and children, were slain! (Ether 15:2). The war continued to rage so furiously that finally there were only two warriors left: Coriantumr and Shiz. In the final battle Shiz was killed; the passage describing Shiz's death contains the following interesting detail: "And it came to pass that after he [Coriantumr] had smitten off the head of Shiz, that Shiz raised upon his hands and fell; and after that he had struggled for breath, he died" (Ether 15:31). Coriantumr, though seriously wounded in this battle, survived and lived with the people of Zarahemla for "nine moons" (Omni 21). The only other survivor of the Jaredites was the prophet Ether, who recorded the history of his people on twenty-four plates. Thus the Jaredites were completely obliterated from North America.

The second, and more important, immigration to America was that of Lehi and his descendants. Lehi, a Jewish prophet of the tribe of Manasseh, was forced to leave Jerusalem in 600 B.C. because of persecution occasioned by his testimony against the wickedness of the Jews and his prediction of the impending destruction of Jerusalem. Lehi, his wife, and his four sons therefore left Jerusalem and went to live in the region bordering on the Red Sea. In obedience to God's command Lehi's sons were sent back to Jerusalem in order to obtain from a certain Laban a set of brass plates containing the five books of Moses, various prophecies, and Lehi's genealogy (the so-called Brass Plates of Laban). As Lehi and his sons journeyed on, they came to the shore of the ocean, where Nephi, one of the sons, proceeded to build a ship in response to a divine revelation telling him to do so. The entire group now entered the ship and began to sail eastward, with the aid of a ball containing a spindle which pointed out the way in which they should go, which Lehi had previously found on the ground (I Nephi 16:10).[44] In course of time they landed on the west coast of South America. (By this time the Jaredites had exterminated themselves.)

Of the sons of Lehi the most prominent were Nephi and Laman. The family of Laman and that of his brother Lemuel were continually in rebellion against the Lord and against His commandments; consequently the Lord cursed them and caused "a skin of blackness" to come upon them (II Nephi 5:21). Since the Lamanites, as the descendants of Laman are called, were the ancestors of the American Indians, it is evident that, according to Mormon teaching, the American Indians are not of the Mongolian race — as most anthropologists declare — but are actually dark-skinned Israelites of the tribe of Manasseh.[45]

The other descendants of Lehi, however, who had begun to call themselves Nephites (after Nephi, whom they recognized as their king), did not rebel against God's commandments. Gradually the Nephites migrated to Central and North America. Here they founded a great civilization and built large cities. In A.D., 34 in fulfillment of a prophecy made earlier by Nephi (I Nephi 12:6ff.), the Lord Jesus Christ Himself came down from heaven, prescribed baptism by immersion, called and commissioned twelve disciples, instituted the sacrament of bread and wine, and uttered many teachings, including virtually the entire Sermon on the Mount (III Nephi 11:28). Though at the time of Christ's appearance all the inhabitants of the land were converted (IV Nephi 2), and though there was peace and harmony between the Lamanites and the Nephites for two hundred years (IV Nephi 17ff.), after this period hostility again arose between these two groups, and there was constant warfare. In A.D. 385 the two groups assembled for a final battle near the hill Cumorah (located by present-day Mormons in upper New York State). In

---

[44] One of the more obvious anachronisms of the *Book of Mormon*. The mariner's compass was not invented until the 12th century A.D.

[45] See Talmage, *Articles of Faith*, pp. 260, 284. One wonders why, if this is the case, the skin of the Lamanites is said to have turned *black*. A Mormon missionary once answered this question by saying that in the days when the plates on which the *Book of Mormon* is based were written there was no word for brown! One would expect, however, that the "inspired translation" would correct this detail. The implications of this teaching about the origin of dark-pigmented skin are rather unflattering to these races, to say the least. It is also interesting to note that, according to Mormon teaching, "when the Lamanites fully repent and sincerely receive the gospel, the Lord has promised to remove the dark skin" (Joseph Fielding Smith, *Answers to Gospel Questions*, III, 123).

this battle the Lamanites killed all the Nephites except one —
Moroni, whose father's name had been Mormon.

Mormon had been writing down the history of his people, the
Nephites, on golden plates. The process of recording this
history had begun with Nephi, the son of Lehi, and had been
continued by other Nephite historians. Nephi had begun en-
graving two kinds of plates: larger plates, containing a secular
history of the Nephites, and smaller plates, containing their
spiritual history. Mormon, who lived in the fourth century A.D.,
had abridged the larger plates of Nephi and had added to this
abridgment the smaller plates of Nephi *in toto*. This entire
collection of golden plates Mormon hid in the hill Cumorah
before the battle of Cumorah. After the battle, Moroni, the
only Nephite survivor, added some additional plates, containing
the books of Ether and Moroni, and buried them also in the hill
Cumorah. This happened in A.D. 421. Fourteen hundred
years later, so Mormons claim, in the years 1823-27, Moroni,
now changed into an angel (though he is sometimes called a
resurrected being), appeared to Joseph Smith, told him where
the plates were hidden, and permitted him to take them.

In the Appendix the question of the genuineness of the *Book
of Mormon* will be taken up in greater detail. Suffice it here
to note that this book is not only recognized by Mormons as
the word of God alongside of the Bible, but is actually thought
to be superior to the Bible. For proof of the latter statement,
the reader is reminded of what is said by Mormons about the
imperfections inherent in all Bible translations and the lack of
these imperfections in the *Book of Mormon,* and also about the
many "plain and precious things" which have been removed from
the Bible. Note also the following statement by Joseph Smith:
"I told the brethren that the Book of Mormon was the most
correct of any book on earth, and the keystone of our religion,
and a man would get nearer to God by abiding by its precepts, than
by any other book."[46] "Any other book" obviously includes
the Bible. Here, therefore, in the words of their inspired "prophet,"
Mormons claim that they have a sacred book which can bring
one nearer to God than even the Bible itself. It may be pre-
sumed, therefore, that if there should be disagreement between

[46] Statement made by Smith on November 28, 1841. Reproduced in
Teachings of the Prophet Joseph Smith, ed. Joseph Fielding Smith (Salt
Lake City: Deseret Book Co., 1958), p. 194.

the King James Version of the Bible and the *Book of Mormon,*
Mormons would follow the latter in preference to the former.

OTHER SACRED BOOKS

In addition to the *Book of Mormon,* however, Mormons recognize two other sacred books. These are actually more important
doctrinally than the *Book of Mormon,* since they contain some of
the most distinctive doctrines of present-day Mormonism. The
first of these is *Doctrine and Covenants.* This volume, which was
first published in its present form in 1876, contains 136 sections
or chapters, each of which is divided into verses. These sections all
contain revelations alleged to have been given through Joseph
Smith, except for Section 136, which was a revelation given through
President Brigham Young. The current version of *Doctrine and
Covenants* also includes the Manifesto prohibiting polygamy issued
by President Wilford Woodruff in 1890. These "revelations" deal
with such doctrines as the nature of God, the church, the priesthood, the millennium, the resurrection, the state of man after death,
the various grades of salvation, and so on. Many of these "revelations" are addressed to specific persons, and deal with very specific
matters. So, for example, Section 19 is addressed to Martin Harris
and instructs him to "pay the debt thou hast contracted with the
printer" (v. 35). In Section 104 a "revelation" is given concerning
the disposition of certain lots and houses in Kirtland, Ohio, along
with the individuals to whom these properties are assigned (vv.
20-46). In Section 132, the famous section on plural marriage,
a specific word is addressed to Joseph Smith's wife, telling her
that she must stand ready to receive the additional wives that
have been given to her husband, on pain of everlasting destruction (vv. 52-54). The particular significance of *Doctrine and
Covenants* for present-day Mormonism is that it contains revelations about baptism for the dead (Sections 124, 127, 128), about
celestial marriage (Section 132, vv. 19 and 20), and about
plural marriage or polygamy (132:61, 62; cf. the Woodruff
Manifesto, pp. 256-257). The *Book of Mormon,* it should be
observed at this point, says nothing about either baptism for
the dead or celestial marriage, and denounces polygamy as a
practice abominable in the sight of the Lord (Jacob 2:24, 27).

The second of these additional sacred books is the *Pearl of
Great Price,* a small volume containing the following writings:
(1) The Book of Moses, a work of eight chapters covering the

same general period as that covered by the first six chapters of Genesis. This book, as was previously indicated, is a copy of the opening chapters of Smith's "Inspired Version" of the Bible; its contents have been described above (see p. 20). (2) The Book of Abraham, purporting to be a translation from an Egyptian papyrus. This document, representing a later stage in Smith's theological development, clearly teaches polytheism, rewriting the first chapter of Genesis in polytheistic fashion: "And they (the Gods) said: Let there be light" (4:3). This book, supposedly written by Abraham while he was in Egypt, tells about the star Kolob, which is said to be the greatest of all the stars and the one nearest to God (3:3, 9, 16), about the pre-existence of souls (3:22), about the plan to prepare an earth for these souls (3:24), about the plan to subject these souls to a period of probation on earth (3:25), and about the organization of matter whereby the heavens and the earth were formed (4:1).[47] (3) An extract from Joseph Smith's translation of the Bible (Chapter 24 of Matthew). (4) Extracts from the History of Joseph Smith, the Prophet — the section of Smith's autobiography which narrates the discovery of the plates and the translation of them. (5) The Articles of Faith.

FURTHER REVELATIONS

Such, then, are the Mormon sacred books. Even these additional writings, however, do not mark the end of divine revelations for Mormons. In *Doctrine and Covenants* 107 the office of president of the church is described as follows:

> And again, the duty of the President of the office of the High Priesthood is to preside over the whole church, and to be like unto Moses — Behold, here is wisdom; yea, to be a seer, a revelator, a translator, and a prophet, having all the gifts of God which he bestows upon the head of the church (vv. 91, 92).

It is also stated by a prominent Mormon author, however, that the counselors to the president, the Council of Twelve Apostles, and usually the Patriarch of the Church are likewise sustained as

---

[47] It will be observed that the Mormons thus have three official accounts of creation: the one found in the King James Version of the Bible; the one found in Chapter 2 of the Book of Moses, which gives the creation story in the first person; and the one found in Chapter 4 of the Book of Abraham, which teaches polytheism. One wonders which account is now to be considered the most authoritative.

"prophets, seers, and revelators."[48]   This same author explains that the revelations received by officers lower than the president of the church (and here he includes bishops and stake presidents as well as those mentioned above) concern the duties of their particular offices; only the president of the church can receive revelations for the guidance of the church as a whole.[49]

Summing up, we have observed that Mormons do not at all accept the Bible as their final authority for doctrine and life; they relegate the Bible to an inferior place of authority.   Their own emendations of the Bible and their own sacred scriptures are considered to be superior in value to the Bible.   In fact, even their president is believed to possess the power of receiving further revelations which could conceivably alter the doctrines accepted by the Mormon Church.

We must at this point assert, in the strongest possible terms, that Mormonism does not deserve to be called a Christian religion. It is basically anti-Christian and anti-Biblical.   The Mormon contention that "after the book [the Bible] hath gone forth through the hands of the great and abominable church . . . there are many plain and precious things taken away from the book. . ." (I Nephi 13:28), is completely contrary to fact.   The many copies of Old Testament manuscripts which we now possess do vary in minor matters — the spelling of words, the omission of a phrase here and there — but there is no evidence whatsoever that any major sections of Old Testament books have been lost. The manuscripts found among the Dead Sea Scrolls, generally dated from about 200 to 50 B.C., include portions of every Old Testament book except Esther; studies have revealed that these documents — older by a thousand years than previously discovered Old Testament manuscripts — are substantially identical to the text of the Old Testament which had been previously handed down.   As far as New Testament manuscripts are concerned, the oldest of which go back to the second century A.D., the situation is substantially the same.   The variations that are found in these manuscripts — all copies of the originals or of copies made from the originals — are of a relatively minor nature.   There is no indication whatever that any large sections of material found in the originals have been lost.   Most of the manuscript variations concern matters of spelling, word order,

---

[48] Widtsoe, *Evidences and Reconciliations,* p. 256.
[49] *Ibid.,* pp. 101, 102.

tense, and the like; no single doctrine is affected by them in any way.[50]   There is, further, not a shred of evidence to show that any translations of the Bible, including the fourth-century Vulgate, which became the official medieval Roman Catholic version, omitted any portions of these manuscripts or failed to reproduce any major sections of the Bible.

The Bible itself, moreover, clearly indicates that it is the final revelation of God to man, and that it does not need to be supplemented by additional revelation.   We have already noted Christ's reference to Moses and the prophets as giving sufficient revelation for man's salvation (Lk. 16:19-31; see above, p. 23). When the risen Christ appeared to the disciples from Emmaus, He did not find it necessary to give them additional revelations, but "beginning from Moses and from all the prophets, he interpreted to them in all the Scriptures the things concerning himself" (Lk. 24:27).   The finality of the revelation that came through Jesus Christ is strikingly expressed in Hebrews 1:1 and 2:

> God, having of old times spoken unto the fathers in the prophets, by divers portions and in divers manners, hath at the end of these days spoken unto us in his Son. . . .

God's revelation through Christ is here described as climactic and definitive — the claim that further revelations would have to be given to the church 1800 years later by Joseph Smith clearly contradicts the thrust of this passage!

The question might be asked: If Jesus Christ was the culmination of God's revelation to man, why was it necessary for the apostles to write the Bible books which have become incorporated into our present New Testament?   The answer is that the apostles had to present to the world their witness to Jesus Christ, so that we might believe on Him on the basis of their testimony.   The purpose of the apostolic witness is well expressed by the Apostle John:

> That which was from the beginning, that which we have heard, that which we have seen with our eyes, that which we beheld, and our hands handled, concerning the word of life (and the life was manifested, and we have seen, and bear witness, and declare unto you the life, the eternal life, which was with the Father, and was manifested unto us); that which we have seen and heard declare we unto you also, that ye also

---

[50] For more technical information on these matters, cf. books on textual criticism like Frederick Kenyon's *Our Bible and the Ancient Manuscripts*, rev. by A. W. Adams (New York: Harper, 1958).

may have fellowship with us: yea, and our fellowship is with
the Father, and with his Son Jesus Christ (I Jn. 1:1-3).

This testimony having been given by the apostles of the first
century after Christ, what need is there for an additional testimony by someone living in the nineteenth century? Our Lord
Himself taught that the word of the apostles was to be sufficient
to lead men to faith: "Neither for these only [the apostles] do I
pray, but for them also [all other believers] that believe on me
through their word" (Jn. 17:20). The Bible further indicates
that the entire church is "built upon the foundation of the apostles
and prophets" (Eph. 2:20). In this passage the word *prophets*
stands for the chief Old Testament agents of revelation, and the
word *apostles,* for the chief New Testament agents of revelation.
Since these two groups constitute the foundation of the church, the
need for the work of another prophet arising eighteen centuries
later is definitely excluded.

In Revelation 22:18 and 19 the following statement is made:

> I [Jesus Christ] testify unto every man that heareth the words
> of the prophecy of this book, If any man shall add unto them,
> God shall add unto him the plagues which are written in this
> book: and if any man shall take away from the words of the
> book of this prophecy, God shall take away his part from the
> tree of life, and out of the holy city, which are written in this
> book.

It must be granted at once that these words apply specifically to
the Book of Revelation to which they are appended. If one
adds to the words of this book, Jesus here says, God shall add to
him the plagues which are written in the book. One may ask
at this juncture whether Section 76 of *Doctrine and Covenants,*
which purports to give further revelations about the three kinds
of heavenly blessedness, is not an adding to the Book of Revelation. Furthermore, note that these words of Jesus set forth in
unmistakable terms the finality and inviolability of a book of the
Bible. The question may well be asked whether these words do
not, by implication, also teach the finality and inviolability of
the other books of the Bible. If one may not add anything to
the Book of Revelation, on what ground is it permissible to
add material to other Biblical books?

In answer to the Mormon contention that a church without
further revelation is a church completely without divine guidance,
we may say that Christ has promised to be with His church always,
even to the end of the world (Mt. 28:20); and that the Holy

Spirit has been given to the church forever (Jn. 14:16), by whose guidance the church continues to live and work. This constant leading of the Spirit, however, does not necessitate the production of new sacred books, since the Spirit now guides the church by means of the inscripturated Word.

I conclude by stating once again that by adding to the Holy Scriptures their additional sacred books, the Mormons have undermined and overthrown "the faith which was once for all delivered unto the saints" (Jude 3).

III. Doctrines

We proceed now to examine the doctrines of Mormonism, following the order of the customary divisions of theology: God, man, Christ, salvation, the church, the last things. Since I am concerned to be as fair and objective as possible in setting forth these doctrines, I shall base this exposition exclusively on Mormon sources.[51]

DOCTRINE OF GOD

THE BEING OF GOD

Mormonism Denies the Trinity. Mormonism teaches that the Persons of the Trinity are not three Persons in one Being, as historic Christianity has always taught, but three separate Beings. Here, at the very outset of our doctrinal discussion, we encounter one of the baffling aspects of Mormon theology: its inconsistency. One may find, for example, many statements in Mormon sacred writings which affirm the unity of God; statements of this sort, however, are nullified by later "revelations" which affirm that Father, Son, and Holy Spirit are three distinct Beings.

The *Book of Mormon,* for example, clearly teaches the doctrine of the Trinity in agreement with historic Christianity: "And now, behold, this is the doctrine of Christ, and the only and true doctrine of the Father, and of the Son, and of the Holy

---

[51] In what follows, I shall not attempt to refute, point by point, the various unscriptural elements in these doctrines, but shall generally try to set forth, with some degree of thoroughness, the doctrinal teachings of Mormonism.

36

Ghost, which is one God, without end" (II Nephi 31:21).
". . . Every thing shall be restored to its perfect frame . . . and
shall be brought and be arraigned before the bar of Christ the
Son, and God the Father, and the Holy Spirit, which is one
eternal God . . ." (Alma 11:44).   Note also the concluding
sentence of the *Testimony of Three Witnesses*: "And the
honor be to the Father, and to the Son, and to the Holy Ghost,
which is one God."   Compare now with the preceding the following statements, made by Joseph Smith in 1844:

> I will preach on the plurality of Gods. I have selected this
> text [Rev. 1:6, in the King James Version] for that express
> purpose. I wish to declare I have always and in all congrega-
> tions when I have preached on the subject of the Deity, it has
> been the plurality of Gods. . . .
>
> I have always declared God to be a distinct personage, Jesus
> Christ a separate and distinct personage from God the Father,
> and that the Holy Ghost was a distinct personage and a Spirit:
> and these three constitute three distinct personages and three
> Gods. . . .
>
> Many men say there is one God; the Father, the Son and the
> Holy Ghost are only one God. I say that is a strange God
> anyhow — three in one, and one in three! It is a curious
> organization. . . . All are to be crammed into one God, ac-
> cording to sectarianism. It would make the biggest God in all
> the world. He would be a wonderfully big God — he would be
> a giant or a monster.[52]

At this juncture we face a real problem. Joseph Smith himself
once said that the *Book of Mormon* was the most correct of any
book on earth (see above, p. 29). In the light of Smith's later
revelation, however, the *Book of Mormon* is here revealed as
having been in error, since it contains the "sectarian" teaching
that God is one. We must challenge Mormons at this point either
to retract Smith's later statement, and thus to admit that their
prophet was in error, or to acknowledge that the *Book of Mormon*
was in error in affirming the unity of God. Mormons have no
right to maintain the errorlessness of both the *Book of Mormon*
and Joseph Smith.

Mormonism Denies the Spirituality of God. "The Father has
a body of flesh and bones as tangible as man's; the Son also; but

---

[52] Sermon on "The Christian Godhead — Plurality of Gods," delivered
on June 16, 1844; quoted in *Teachings of the Prophet Joseph Smith*, pp.
370, 372.

the Holy Ghost has not a body of flesh and bones, but is a personage of Spirit" (*Doctrine and Covenants* 130:22). Thus, though an exception is made in the case of the Holy Spirit, it is clearly taught that both Father and Son have material bodies. ". . . It is clear that the Father is a personal being, possessing a definite form, with bodily parts and spiritual passions."[53] In fact, this same author goes on to say, "We affirm that to deny the materiality of God's person is to deny God; for a thing without parts has no whole, and an immaterial body cannot exist."[54] One wonders at this juncture how Mormons can believe that the Holy Spirit exists. If "an immaterial body cannot exist," how can the Holy Spirit exist, who "has not a body of flesh and bones"? To be consistent, Mormons should deny either the existence of the Holy Spirit or the truth of the Talmage statement last quoted.

The fact that, according to Mormons, God has a material body (with the exception of the Holy Spirit) implies that sex distinctions must also apply to God. This is what is actually taught in the Mormon sacred scriptures: "In the image of his own body, male and female, created he them . . ." (Book of Moses 6:9). John A. Widtsoe, a prominent Mormon author, puts it this way: "In accordance with Gospel philosophy there are males and females in heaven. Since we have a Father, who is our God, we must also have a mother, who possesses the attributes of Godhood."[55] This thought, that we have a mother in heaven as well as a father, is given poetic expression in the third stanza of a well-known Mormon hymn, "O my Father":

> I had learned to call thee Father,
>   Through Thy Spirit from on high;
> But, until the key of Knowledge
>   Was restored, I knew not why.
> In the heavens are parents single?
>   No; the thought makes reason stare!
> Truth is reason; truth eternal
>   Tells me, I've a mother there.[56]

Mormonism Teaches That There Are a Great Many Gods in Addition to Father, Son, and Holy Spirit. The first thing we

[53] James E. Talmage, *Articles of Faith,* p. 41.
[54] *Ibid.,* p. 48.
[55] *A Rational Theology,* 6th ed. (Salt Lake City: Deseret Book Co., 1952), p. 69.
[56] Quoted from Ben E. Rich, *Mr. Durant of Salt Lake City* (Salt Lake City: Deseret News Press, 1952), p. 77.

should note is that here again we see a certain evolution in Mormon doctrinal teachings. In the Book of Moses, allegedly revealed to Joseph Smith in 1830, the first chapter of Genesis is reproduced with the name of God in the singular: "And I, God, said: Let there be light; and there was light" (2:3; see rest of chapter). In the Book of Abraham, however, supposedly translated in the summer of 1835,[57] the first chapter of Genesis is reproduced again, this time with the name of God in the plural: "And they (the Gods) said: Let there be light; and there was light" 4:3); the plural form, Gods, continues throughout the remainder of this chapter, as well as throughout Chapter 5. If we are to receive the later revelation as the more authoritative, it would appear that the earlier revelation, which spoke of God in the singular, was in error.

Smith tried to justify this translation of the creation account by pointing out that the Hebrew word usually translated God, *Elohim,* is in the plural.[58] Though this is true, the plural as it here occurs is recognized by all Hebrew scholars as a plural of majesty, referring to the one true God.[59] The very fact that the Hebrew verb forms which have *Elohim* as their subject are almost invariably in the singular number proves that the author of Genesis intended to speak of a single God and not of a plurality of gods.

In the sermon on "The Christian Godhead — Plurality of Gods" previously referred to, Joseph Smith declared:

> . . . The doctrine of a plurality of gods is as prominent in the Bible as any other doctrine. It is all over the face of the Bible. It stands beyond the power of controversy. A wayfaring man, though a fool, need not err therein.
>
> Paul says there are Gods many and Lords many. I want to set it forth in a plain and simple manner; but to us there is but one God — that is, *pertaining to us.* . . .
>
> The heads of the Gods appointed one God for us; and when you take [that] view of the subject, it sets one free to see all the beauty, holiness and perfection of the Gods.[60]

It is quite clear from these statements that, according to Smith's

57 Joseph Fielding Smith, *Essentials in Church History,* p. 184.
58 *Teachings of the Prophet Joseph Smith,* p. 371.
59 See, for example, Francis Brown, S. R. Driver, and Charles A. Briggs, *Hebrew and English Lexicon of the Old Testament* (Boston: Houghton Mifflin, 1907), p. 43.
60 *Teachings of the Prophet Joseph Smith,* pp. 370, 372.

latest revelations, there are a great many gods, but that one god has been appointed particularly for the people who inhabit this earth.

To the same effect are statements attributed to Brigham Young, the second president of the church, who, according to Mormon teaching, was also a "revelator" and therefore also spoke with infallible authority.   The following pronouncement is very clear in its implications:

> How many Gods there are, I do not know. But there never was a time when there were not Gods and worlds, and when men were not passing through the same ordeals that we are now passing through. That course has been from all eternity, and it is and will be to all eternity.[61]

According to this passage, the world we live in is not the only world there is, but there have been a great number of worlds and also a great number of gods.

From a more recent Mormon author we learn that there has been an infinite succession of gods which have come into being through a process of generation: "The Prophet taught that our Father had a Father and so on. Is this not a reasonable thought, especially when we remember that the promises are made to us that we may become like him?"[62]   An illuminating discussion of the relation of these various gods to each other will be found in Chapter 12 of John A. Widtsoe's *A Rational Theology*. From this chapter we learn that the various gods are in an order of progression, that there are some in almost every conceivable stage of development, that God, angel, and similar terms "denote merely intelligent beings of varying degree of development" (p. 66), and that God the Father is simply the supreme God — that is, the god who has reached the highest stage of development. The difference between angels and gods is thus one of degree, and that between God the Father and the other gods is likewise one of degree. He is simply the god who has progressed the farthest and is therefore superior to the other gods — the other gods will never be able to catch up with him. Mormonism thus embraces a polytheism of the rankest kind.

Mormonism Also Teaches That the Gods Were Once Men. In his famous King Follett Discourse, delivered in 1844 at the

---

[61] *Discourses of Brigham Young,* arranged by John A. Widtsoe (Salt Lake City: Deseret Book Co., 1954), pp. 22-23.
[62] Joseph Fielding Smith, *Doctrines of Salvation,* I, 12.

funeral of Elder King Follett, Joseph Smith made the following statement:

> God himself was once as we are now, and is an exalted man, and sits enthroned in yonder heavens! . . . If you were to see him today, you would see him like a man in form. . . . He was once a man like us; yea . . . God himself, the Father of us all, dwelt on an earth, the same as Jesus Christ himself did. . . .[63]

Smith does not tell us when the Father dwelt on an earth; the expression "an earth," in fact, suggests that he dwelt on a different earth than the one we inhabit. To the same effect is the following statement by a Mormon writer:

> Mormon prophets have continuously taught the sublime truth that God the Eternal Father was once a mortal man who passed through a school of earth life similar to that through which we are now passing. He became God — an exalted being — through obedience to the same eternal Gospel truths that we are given opportunity today to obey.[64]

It is quite obvious from these quotations that Mormons flatly deny such distinctively Christian doctrines as the immutability of God, the eternity of God, and the transcendence of God — His absolute distinctness from man. What their view amounts to is that all gods first existed as spirits, came to an earth to receive bodies, and then, after having passed through a period of probation on the aforesaid earth, were advanced to the exalted position they now enjoy in some heavenly realm. When commenting on the thought that God is said to exist from eternity to eternity, Joseph Fielding Smith observes: "From eternity to eternity means from the spirit existence through the probation which we are in, and then back again to the eternal existence which will follow."[65] Thus every god has passed through a cycle similar to that which we observe in the incarnation of Jesus Christ. The uniqueness of Christ's incarnation is thus completely repudiated.

Mormonism Teaches That Men May Become Gods. In the same King Follett Discourse to which reference has just been made, Joseph Smith said,

> Here, then, is eternal life — to know the only wise and true God; and you have got to learn how to be Gods yourselves,

---

[63] *Teachings of the Prophet Joseph Smith,* pp. 345-46.
[64] Milton R. Hunter, *The Gospel through the Ages* (Salt Lake City: Deseret Book Co., 1958), p. 104.
[65] *Doctrines of Salvation,* I, 12.

and to be kings and priests to God, the same as all Gods have done before you, namely, by going from one small degree to another, and from a small capacity to a great one; from grace to grace, from exaltation to exaltation, until you attain to the resurrection of the dead, and are able to dwell in everlasting burnings, and to sit in glory, as do those who sit enthroned in everlasting power.[66]

This extremely blunt and much criticized statement, however, is only a logical development of what is found in *Doctrine and Covenants,* Chapter 132. In verse 37 of this section we are told that Abraham and the other patriarchs, because they did what they were commanded, now sit upon thrones and are not angels but gods. In verses 19 and 20 of this chapter, furthermore, we are taught that those who shall marry according to the new and everlasting covenant, whereby they are sealed to their spouses for eternity, shall after this life become gods.

That this is still accepted Mormon teaching is shown in the following statement by Joseph Fielding Smith: ". . . We have to pass through mortality and receive the resurrection and then go on to perfection just as our Father did before us."[67] Lorenzo Snow, fifth president of the Mormon Church, expressed this same truth epigrammatically: "As man is, God once was; as God is, man may become."[68] Widtsoe sums the matter up very neatly when he tell us, "In short, man is a god in embryo."[69]

According to Mormonism, therefore, man is a god in the making. He, too, was once a spirit-creature; he then came to this earth to receive a physical tabernacle; after a period of earthly probation he dies and is raised again; if he has passed the probation, he shall gradually advance to the status of godhood. In Mormon theology, therefore, not only is God dragged down to the level of man, but man is at the same time exalted to potential deity. All ultimate differentiation between God and man has been done away with in this system, which now promises to its adherents what Satan, through the serpent, once promised to Eve: "Ye shall be as God" (Gen. 3:5).

In this connection, something should be said about the so-called "Adam-God theory." The following statement by President Brigham Young has often been quoted:

[66] *Teachings of the Prophet Joseph Smith,* pp. 346-47.
[67] *Doctrines of Salvation,* I, 12.
[68] *Millennial Star,* 54, 404; quoted in Hunter, *op. cit.,* pp. 105-106.
[69] *A Rational Theology,* p. 26.

> When our father Adam came into the Garden of Eden, he
> came into it with a celestial body, and brought Eve, one of his
> wives, with him. He helped to make and organize this world.
> He is Michael, the Archangel, the Ancient of Days, about
> whom holy men have written and spoken — He is our father
> and our God, and the only God with whom we have to do.[70]

By many non-Mormons this statement has been understood as implying that Adam was identical with God the Father (*Elohim*).
Joseph Fielding Smith, however, goes to great lengths to indicate
that President Young's statement should not be thus understood.
Referring to passages in *Doctrine and Covenants* in which Adam
is called Michael and is said to have been the Ancient of Days
(27:11; 78:15-16), Smith insists that Young only meant to say
that Adam was the pre-existent spirit known as Michael, who
helped Elohim and Jehovah (another name for Christ) form this
earth.   Adam also became the father of the physical bodies
of the members of the human race, and was given the keys of
salvation.   Hence the human family is immediately subject to
Adam.   It is in this sense that Adam may be thought of as "the
only god with whom we have to do."   This does not mean,
however, Smith continues, that Adam is to be identified with
God the Father.[71]

One may well question whether Joseph Fielding Smith has interpreted Brigham Young correctly.   After all, the statement, "He is
our father and our God, and the only God with whom we have
to do," seems hard to fit into the type of interpretation Smith
advances.   If, however, we accept Smith's interpretation as representing the current Mormon view, we get this picture: Adam was
a spirit who was pre-existent as the Archangel Michael.   In this
pre-existent state he must have had a number of wives, since Eve
is called "one of his wives."   He helped God the Father and
Jesus Christ make and organize this earth.   He was then placed
on this earth, and was given a physical body, so that he and
Eve (who was also given a body) could become the progenitors
of the physical bodies of the members of the human race (whose
spirits had been previously begotten by Elohim).   Adam was
also given the keys of salvation, and he was assigned dominion
over every living creature.   On account of these facts, Adam

---

[70] *Journal of Discourses,* I, 50; quoted in Smith, *Doctrines of Salvation,*
I, 96.
[71] *Doctrines of Salvation,* I, 96-101.

may be recognized as "a god" — as one to whom we are to be subject. Yet Adam is subordinate to Jesus Christ, and Christ is, in turn, subordinate to God the Father (Elohim). It is specifically stated that Mormons do not worship Adam or pray to him, but that they worship Elohim.[72]

To suggest that Adam is a god is, however, in gross contradiction to the Scriptures, which teach us that Adam was the first created man, the father of the human race, through whose fall into sin all men have come under condemnation (Rom. 5:12-21). The suggestion that Adam is to be looked up to as a god robs the fall of all its seriousness, and obliterates completely the distinction between the Creator and the creature.

THE WORKS OF GOD

Decrees. It can hardly be expected that Mormons, with their view of the plurality of gods and of the changeableness of God, could have anything resembling the historic Reformed doctrine of predestination. We find, accordingly, that Mormon writers are extremely critical of this doctrine:

> Predestination is the false doctrine that from all eternity God has ordered whatever comes to pass, having especial and particular reference to the salvation or damnation of souls. Some souls, according to this false concept, are irrevocably chosen for salvation, others for damnation; and there is said to be nothing any individual can do to escape his predestined inheritance in heaven or in hell as the case may be.[73]

McConkie insists, however, that Mormons do believe in foreordination: "To carry forward his own purposes among men and nations, the Lord *foreordained* chosen spirit children in pre-existence and assigned them to come to earth at particular times and places so that they might aid in furthering the divine will."[74] He then goes on to show, from both Mormon and Christian Scrip-

---

[72] *Ibid.*, p. 106. Not all Mormons would agree with Smith's interpretation of Brigham Young's words, however. In 1950 W. Gordon Hackney, a faculty member at Brigham Young University published a pamphlet of twenty-two pages entitled *That Adam-God Doctrine,* in which he vigorously defended the teaching that Adam is our Heavenly Father, and that Adam and Eve were the parents, not only of our physical bodies, but also of our spirits in the pre-existent world.

[73] Bruce R. McConkie, *Mormon Doctrine,* p. 530. Similar sentiments are expressed by Joseph Fielding Smith in an article entitled "Apostate Doctrine of Predestination" (*Doctrines of Salvation,* III, 286).

[74] McConkie, *op. cit.,* p. 269.

tures, that the following were foreordained to their spiritual call-
ings: Joseph Smith, Abraham, Jeremiah, Christ, Mary, John the
Baptist, and all holders of the Melchizedek priesthood. He makes
it very clear, however, that there is no compulsion involved in
this foreordination, but that persons who are so foreordained retain their free agency. "By their foreordination the Lord merely
gives them the opportunity to serve him and his purposes if they
will choose to measure up to the standard he knows they are
capable of attaining."[75]

From this and other discussions of predestination by Mormon
writers, it becomes quite evident that these authors do not understand what this doctrine really teaches. Interpreting predestination as tantamount to fatalism, they reject it. If, however, the
foreordination which they teach really means nothing more than
an opportunity to serve the Lord, one wonders what is the real
difference between this foreordination and the invitation to salvation which, so they affirm, comes to all men.[76] If, on the other
hand, there is a real foreordination of these individuals to the
tasks for which they have been chosen, this must be more than a
mere opportunity for service. The Mormon doctrine of foreordination does justice neither to the sovereignty of God nor to
the certainty of planned events, as taught in Scripture. Was the
Lamb "slain from the foundation of the world" (Rev. 13:8)
merely given an *opportunity* to die on the cross?

Creation. Mormonism rejects the doctrine of creation out of
nothing, or *ex nihilo,* affirming that what the Bible calls creation was simply a reorganization of matter which had always
existed. Note the following statement from *Doctrine and Covenants*: "For man is spirit. The elements are eternal, and spirit
and element, inseparably connected, receive a fulness of joy. . ."
(93:33). The word *elements* here means material elements, as
the following quotation from Smith's King Follett Discourse will
reveal:

> You ask the learned doctors why they say the world was
> made out of nothing; and they will answer, "Doesn't the Bible
> say he *created* the world?" And they infer, from the word
> create, that it must have been made out of nothing. Now, the
> word create came from the word *baurau*, which does not
> mean to create out of nothing; it means to organize; the same

[75] *Ibid.*
[76] LeGrand Richards, *A Marvelous Work and a Wonder* (Salt Lake City;
Deseret Book Co., 1950), pp. 358-61.

as a man would organize materials and build a ship. Hence we infer that God had materials to organize the world out of chaos — chaotic matter, which is element, and in which dwells all the glory. Element had an existence from the time he had. The pure principles of element are principles which can never be destroyed; they may be organized and reorganized, but not destroyed. They had no beginning, and can have no end.[77]

Present-day Mormon writers are committed to this view. Bruce McConkie says, "To *create* is to *organize*. It is an utterly false and uninspired notion to believe that the world or any other thing was created out of nothing. . . ."[78] John A. Widtsoe puts it this way: "God, the supreme Power, cannot conceivably originate matter; he can only organize matter. Neither can he destroy matter; he can only disorganize it."[79]

When we reflect on the fact that the gods were once mortal men, we must come to the conclusion that matter is actually more eternal, at least in origin, than the gods. For the gods did not exist as gods from eternity, but matter did. Furthermore, it would appear that all the gods except the head of the gods had a beginning, for Joseph Smith, in his sermon on the plurality of gods, insisted that the proper translation of Genesis 1:1 was, "In the beginning the head of the Gods brought forth the Gods."[80] Matter, however, as we have just seen, had no beginning. In Mormon theology, therefore, matter is more ultimate than the gods.

Before the gods "created" this earth, or any other earths, they "created" a spirit world. "For I, the Lord God, created all things, of which I have spoken, spiritually, before they were naturally upon the face of the earth" (Moses 3:4). This spirit world, as Joseph Fielding Smith indicates, includes the spirits of all men, but also the "spirits" of animals and plants:

> We were all created untold ages before we were placed on this earth. We discover from Abraham 3:22-28, that it was before the earth was formed that the plan of salvation was presented to the spirits, or "intelligences." This being true, then man, animals and plants were not created in the spirit at the time of the creation of the earth, but long before.[81]

[77] *Teachings of the Prophet Joseph Smith*, pp. 350-52.
[78] *Mormon Doctrine*, p. 156.
[79] *A Rational Theology*, p. 12. Cf. his *Evidences and Reconciliations*, p. 150.
[80] *Teachings of the Prophet Joseph Smith*, p. 371.
[81] *Doctrines of Salvation*, I, 76.

McConkie adds to this the thought that these spirit-creatures had a part in the natural "creation":

> There is no revealed account of the spirit creation. . . . That this prior spirit creation occurred long before the temporal or natural creation is evident from the fact that spirit men, men who themselves were before created spiritually, were participating in the natural creation.[82]

Before the earth on which we live was "created," many other worlds were "created," each with its own inhabitants:

> This earth was not the first of the Lord's creation. An infinite number of worlds have come rolling into existence at his command. Each is called *earth;* each is inhabited with his spirit children; each abides the particular law given to it; and each will play its part in the redemption, salvation, and exaltation of that infinite host of the children of an Almighty God.[83]

In order to understand how this earth was "created," we must note the distinction Mormons make between Elohim and Jehovah. For Mormons Elohim is the name given to "God the eternal Father."[84] Jehovah is, for Mormons, another name for Christ in his pre-incarnate state.[85]

How, now, do Mormons picture the "creation" of this earth? A council of the gods was held on the star Kolob, at which the

---

[82] *Mormon Doctrine*, p. 158.

[83] *Ibid.*, p. 157; cf. Moses 1:29, 35; 7:30.

[84] McConkie, *op. cit.*, p. 207. One wonders, however, whether this Father also had a Father. Joseph Smith once said, "Where was there ever a son without a father? And where was there ever a father without first being a son? . . . Hence if Jesus had a Father, can we not believe that He had a Father also?" (*Teachings of the Prophet Joseph Smith*, p. 373). On the basis of this statement, there can be no end to this infinite regression — every father one can think of must have had a father, and this must hold for the gods as well.

[85] McConkie, *op. cit.*, p. 359. It should be noted here that the distinction Mormons make between Elohim and Jehovah is completely untenable. Mormons are apparently oblivious of the fact that in many Old Testament passages Elohim and Jehovah (or Yahweh) appear together as designating the same being. So, for example, in Gen. 2:7, rendered in the King James: "And the Lord God [Hebrew: Yahweh Elohim] formed man of the dust of the ground. . . ." Cf. Gen. 2:4, 5, 8, 16, 18, 21, 22, and so on. The expression, "the Lord God," appears even in Joseph Smith's Revised Version, and in Chapter 3 of the Book of Moses!

organization of this earth was planned.[86]   The Book of Abraham tells the story: Abraham was shown a number of souls that were in existence before the earth had been formed (3:22, 23).   The book continues:

> And there stood one among them that was like unto God [presumably Christ], and he said unto those who were with him: We will go down, for there is space there, and we will take of these materials, and we will make an earth whereon these may dwell. . . .
> And then the Lord said: Let us go down.   And they went down at the beginning, and they, that is the Gods, organized and formed the heavens and the earth (3:24; 4:1).

The gods labored for six days; each of these days, however, was a thousand years long — since a thousand earth years is equivalent to a day on the star Kolob.[87]

Jesus Christ, or Jehovah, "created" this earth, under the direction of his Father, Elohim.   He was helped in this process by Michael, who was Adam in his pre-existent form.   Joseph Fielding Smith adds: "I have a strong view or conviction that there were others also who assisted them.   Perhaps Noah and Enoch; and *why not Joseph Smith*, and those who were appointed to be rulers before the earth was formed?"[88]   McConkie adds to the group of those who assisted in this "creation" also Abraham, Moses, Peter, James, and John.[89]   The "creation" of this earth was thus a kind of co-operative venture between the gods and the spirits of certain pre-existent men.   One can therefore by no means speak of "creation" in the Mormon sense as exclusively the work of God or the gods — unless one wishes to view these pre-existent human spirits as already gods in the making.

After this earth has passed away, others will be organized, and so on, *ad infinitum*: "And as one earth shall pass away, and the heavens thereof, even so shall another come; and there is no end to my works, neither to my words" (Moses 1:38).

The Providence of God.   It is difficult to see how there can be a real doctrine of divine providence in Mormon theology, since there are so many gods, and since these gods are continually progressing and therefore changing.   The doctrine of providence

---

[86] George Arbaugh, on p. 107 of his *Revelation in Mormonism*, quotes a poem of Joseph Smith's in which he states this fact.

[87] Smith, *Doctrines of Salvation*, I, 78-79.

[88] *Ibid.*, p. 75.   See also p. 74.

[89] *Op. cit.*, p. 157.

does not, in fact, appear to play any prominent part in Mormon thinking about God. Though much is made of God's care for his saints and of his divine direction of their history, we do not find *providence* listed as a major topic in most Mormon doctrinal books. An exception to this rule is the *Doctrine and Covenants Commentary,* which contains a paragraph about the providence of God in a comment on section 3:3, "Remember, remember that it is not the work of God that is frustrated, but the work of men. . . ." In this paragraph God's providence is described as follows: "He [God] preserves and governs all His creatures, and directs their actions, so that the ultimate results will serve the ends He has in view."[90]

One is constrained, however, to raise certain questions: If matter is more eternal than even the highest of the gods (since even the highest god was a man before he became a god), what gives the highest god the right and the power to preserve and govern the material universe? Since the spirits of pre-existent men had a part in the work of "creation," is it not natural to expect that the spirits of other pre-existent men, or the spirits of these same men in their exalted state, should have a part in the work of providence? Since there are many gods, to which god must the work of providence be ascribed? If the work of providence must be ascribed to the highest of the gods, does not this work of providence then include the preservation and government of the other gods as well? If it does not, who preserves and governs them? And if the highest god was once a man as we are now, who was in providential control of the universe at the time this god was only a man? As a matter of fact, if this highest god, as Mormons teach, once dwelt on an earth in the process of becoming a god, and if the earths were all "organized" by gods, where did the earth come from to which the first god had to go before he could become a god?

DOCTRINE OF MAN

MAN IN HIS ORIGINAL STATE

Man's Pre-existence. As we have seen, Mormons teach that before men inhabited this earth, they existed as spirits. Talmage, in fact, sees in this a parallel between our existence and that of

---

[90] Hyrum M. Smith and Janne M. Sjodahl, *Doctrine and Covenants Commentary* (Salt Lake City: Deseret Book Co., 1960), p. 18.

Christ: "Yet Christ was born a child among mortals; and it is consistent to infer that if His earthly birth was the union of a preexistent or antemortal spirit with a mortal body such also is the birth of every member of the human family."[91]   It will be recalled that according to Moses 3:5 all things were "created" spiritually before they were naturally upon the face of the earth.

The question now arises: how did these pre-existent spirits of men originate?   It is quite common to read in Mormon literature that these spirits were begotten by God the Father.   For example, note the following statement from *Doctrine and Covenants*: ". . . By him [the Only Begotten Son], and through him, and of him, the worlds are and were created, and the inhabitants thereof are begotten sons and daughters unto God" (76:24).   To the same effect is the following statement by Brigham Young: "Our Father in Heaven begat all the spirits that ever were, or ever will be, upon this earth; and they were born spirits in the eternal world."[92]   A statement by the First Presidency of the Church (Joseph F. Smith, John R. Winder, Anthon H. Lund) adds the thought that a divine mother was involved in the origin of spirits as well as a divine father:

> "All men and women are in the similitude of the universal Father and Mother, and are literally the sons and daughters of Deity"; as spirits they were the "offspring of celestial parentage."[93]

The foregoing gives one the impression that these pre-existent spirits were begotten and not "created," and that there is hence a real difference between the origin of these spirits and that of the animals or of the earth. Joseph Fielding Smith, in fact, makes precisely this observation in one of his books.[94]   Yet in the Book of Abraham we find the word *organized* used to indicate the way in which these spirits came into existence — and it will be recalled that the word *organized* is the word commonly used to indicate the way in which the earth came to be: "Now the Lord had shown unto me, Abraham, the intelligences that were organized before the world was; and among all these there were many of the

---

[91] *Articles of Faith*, p. 193.
[92] *Discourses of Brigham Young*, p. 24. Cf. Smith, *Doctrines of Salvation*, I, 62-63, 90, 106.
[93] Joseph Fielding Smith, *Man: His Origin and Destiny*, pp. 351, 355; quoted by McConkie, *Mormon Doctrine*, p. 530.
[94] *Doctrines of Salvation*, I, 63.

noble and great ones. . ." (3:22). The word *organized* suggests
that previous to the "begetting" or "organizing" of these spirits
their substance must have been in existence. We would expect to
find Mormons teaching this, since, as we have noted, they repudiate
creation out of nothing. This is precisely what we find in Mormon
writings. Note the following statement from *Doctrine and Covenants*: "Man was also in the beginning with God. Intelligence,
or the light of truth, was not created or made, neither indeed can
be" (93:29). Joseph Fielding Smith puts it this way: "The
intelligent part of man was never created but always existed."[95]
Mr. McConkie, quoting *Doctrine and Covenants* 93:29, interprets
"intelligence" as standing for a "self-existent spirit element":

> Unless God the Father was a personal Being, he could not have
> begotten spirits in his image, and if there had been no self-
> existent spirit element, there would have been no substance
> from which those spirit bodies could have been organized.[96]

In the light of the above it would seem that the begetting of
these pre-existent human spirits means the organization into
"spirit bodies" of self-existent spirit elements which were always
there.[97] Thus there would seem to be two eternally existent sub-
stances: matter and spirit. But, according to *Doctrine and
Covenants*, spirit is only a refined form of matter: "There is no
such thing as immaterial matter. All spirit is matter, but it is
more fine or pure, and can only be discerned by purer eyes. . ."
(131:7). If spirit is only matter which is "more fine or pure,"
one would presume that intelligence is also a purer form of matter.
We conclude that there is only one eternally existent substance:
matter; this substance exists, however, in both a coarse and a
refined form. Where either the matter or the distinction just
alluded to came from, however, Mormons do not divulge.

This pre-existent life was an infinitely long period of "probation, progression, and schooling."[98] All the spirits probably had
an equal start, but some outstripped the others in the quality of

95 *Ibid.,* p. 12.
96 *Mormon Doctrine,* pp. 530-31. By "spirit bodies" Mr. McConkie means
bodies which "were made of a more pure and refined substance than the
elements from which mortal bodies are made."
97 At this point the question cannot be suppressed: If these self-existent
spirit elements always existed, what is the difference between men and
gods, since, as we saw, all the gods except one have also been "brought
forth" by the head of the gods?
98 McConkie, *op. cit.,* p. 531.

their pre-existent life,[99] and became noble and great ones (Abraham 3:22). The reason for the discrimination between races is found in the conduct of spirits in the pre-existent state:

> There is a reason why one man is born black and with other disadvantages, while another is born white with great advantages. The reason is that we once had an estate before we came here, and were obedient, more or less, to the laws that were given us there. Those who were faithful in all things there received greater blessings here, and those who were not faithful received less.[100]

The Image of God. Moses 6:9 reads: "In the image of his own body, male and female, created he them. . . ." This passage makes it quite clear that Mormons understand the expression "image of God" as applying primarily to man's physical nature. LeGrand Richards, in his *A Marvelous Work and a Wonder,* takes issue with those who would understand the image of God as applying only to man's spiritual nature. He insists that the appearance of the Father and the Son in human form to Joseph Smith proved beyond a doubt that God the Father has a body exactly like man's body. He also adduces Genesis 5:3 to establish this point: "And Adam lived an hundred and thirty years, and begat a son in his own likeness, after his image; and called his name Seth." Since in this passage image and likeness must have reference to the body, so Richards argues, the expression "image of God" must have a similar reference (pp. 16-17). The non-Mormon cannot help wondering at this point, however, how the deity of the Holy Spirit can be safeguarded in Mormon theology. It would seem from the above that man is more like God the Father and hence more divine than the Holy Spirit, who has no body at all.

Man's Existence on the Earth. Adam, who before his sojourn on this earth was Michael, the Archangel, received from God a tabernacle of flesh, made from the dust of this earth.[101] Eve, who was also a pre-existent spirit before her incarnation, was likewise given a body by God, and was joined to Adam in the new and everlasting covenant of marriage (Moses 3:20-25). Both Adam and Eve were created with immortal bodies — bodies that

---

[99] Smith, *Doctrines of Salvation,* I, 59.

[100] *Ibid.,* p. 61. Cf. McConkie, *op. cit.,* pp. 476-77.

[101] Smith, *Doctrines of Salvation,* I, 90. On p. 92 the author informs us that though Adam was in the flesh at this time there was no blood in Adam's body before the fall.

were not subject to death (II Nephi 2:22). Mormons claim to have solved the vexing problem of the location of the Garden of Eden. It was located, according to them, in Independence, Missouri — the very place where the New Jerusalem will be built in the latter days.[102]   The reason why the cradle of civilization later moved to the Mesopotamian area, according to Mormons, is that at the time of the Flood Noah's ark was driven by the wind from the American continent to Asia.

MAN IN THE STATE OF SIN

The Fall of Man. Mormons teach that if Adam and Eve had not partaken of the forbidden fruit they would have had no children:

> And now, behold, if Adam had not transgressed he would not have fallen, but he would have remained in the Garden of Eden. . . .
> And they would have had no children; wherefore they would have remained in a state of innocence, having no joy, for they knew no misery; doing no good, for they knew no sin. . . .
> Adam fell that men might be; and men are, that they might have joy (II Nephi 2:22-25).

If this be granted, the fall must have been a good thing, since without it there would have been no human race. It seems hard to understand, however, why marriage was instituted by God before the fall, as Mormons admit.[103]   Apparently, for Mormons, marriage before the fall was not intended as a means for propagating the race.

Eve first disobeyed God by eating of the forbidden fruit. At this juncture Adam found himself in a dilemma. Previously God had commanded him and Eve to multiply and replenish the earth. Since Eve had now fallen into the state of mortality and Adam had not, they were in such dissimilar conditions that they could not remain together. If they should not remain together, however, they would be unable to fulfill God's command to replenish the earth. On the other hand, to yield to Eve's request to eat the fruit would also be tantamount to disobedience. Adam, however, "deliberately and wisely decided to stand by the first and greater commandment; and, therefore, with understanding of the

---

102 *Ibid.,* III, 74.
103 Smith, *Doctrines of Salvation,* I, 115.

nature of his act, he also partook of the fruit. . . ."[104]   Instead of
doing wrong, therefore, Adam really did a wise thing when he
ate the forbidden fruit.

Accordingly, in the Book of Moses we find Adam saying,
"Blessed be the name of God, for because of my transgression
my eyes are opened, and in this life I shall have joy . . ." (5:10).
Eve likewise rejoices at the fall, saying, "Were it not for our
transgression we never should have had seed, and never should
have known good and evil, and the joy of our redemption. . ."
(5:11).   Joseph Fielding Smith, therefore, is only echoing the
Mormon Scriptures when he says, "The fall of man came as a
blessing in disguise, and was the means of furthering the purposes of the Lord in the progress of man, rather than a means
of hindering them."[105]

At this point the question arises: Was the eating of the forbidden fruit sin?   Brigham Young asserts that it was: "How did
Adam and Eve sin?   Did they come out in direct opposition to
God and to his government?   No.   But they transgressed a
command of the Lord, and through that transgression sin came
into the world."[106]   Joseph Fielding Smith, however, prefers not
to speak of Adam's transgression as a sin:

> I never speak of the part Eve took in this fall as a sin,
> nor do I accuse Adam of a sin.   One may say, "Well [,] did
> they not break a commandment?"   Yes.   But let us examine
> the nature of that commandment and the results which came
> out of it.
>
> In no other commandment the Lord ever gave to man, did he
> say: "But of the tree of the knowledge of good and evil, thou
> shalt not eat of it, nevertheless, thou mayest choose for thy-
> self."[107]
>
> It is true, the Lord warned Adam and Eve that to partake of
> the fruit they would transgress a law, and this happened.   But
> it is not always a sin to transgress a law.   I will try to illustrate
> this.   The chemist in his laboratory takes different elements and
> combines them, and the result is that something very different
> results.   He has changed the law. . . .   Well, Adam's transgres-
> sion was of a similar nature, that is, his transgression was in
> accordance with law.[108]

[104] Talmage, *Articles of Faith*, p. 65.
[105] *Doctrines of Salvation*, 1, 114.
[106] *Discourses of Brigham Young*, p. 103.
[107] Quoted from Moses 3:17.   The final clause has been added to the
text by Joseph Smith.
[108] *Doctrines of Salvation*, I, 114.

In the light of the above, therefore, we observe that for Mormons Adam's sin was not really a sin, and the fall was not really a fall. The fall was rather a step upward: a means for providing billions of pre-existent spirits with mortal tabernacles, and a necessary stage in man's ultimate exaltation to godhood. Mormons therefore view Adam not as the one responsible for the curse which now rests upon the earth, but rather as someone for whom they are to be profoundly grateful:

> Father Adam was one of the most noble and intelligent characters who ever lived. . . . He is the head of all gospel dispensations, the presiding high priest (under Christ) over all the earth; presides over all the spirits destined to inhabit this earth; holds the keys of salvation over all the earth; and will reign as Michael, our prince, to all eternity.[109]
> We, the children of Adam and Eve, may well be proud of our parentage.[110]

It can be understood that this view of the fall has profoundly affected Mormon theology. By this reinterpretation of the significance of the fall, Mormons have repudiated the deep seriousness of Adam's sin and have minimized the importance of the work of Christ. Instead of contrasting Adam with Christ, as the Scriptures do (see Rom. 5:12-21), Mormons place Adam alongside of Christ as one who played a role almost as important as that of Christ in enabling man to reach his exaltation.

Original Sin. Article 2 of the Mormon Articles of Faith reads as follows: "We believe that men will be punished for their own sins, and not for Adam's transgression." Mormons, therefore, do not accept the doctrine of original sin. Talmage explains that bodily weakness, disease, and death have come into the world because of the disobedience of Adam and Eve, but that we are not accounted sinners because of the transgression of our first parents.[111]

Mormons further teach the complete sinlessness of infants: "Every spirit of man was innocent in the beginning; and God having redeemed man from the fall, men became again, in their infant state, innocent before God" (*Doctrine and Covenants* 93:38). Joseph Smith had a vision in the year 1836 in which

---

109 McConkie, *op. cit.*, p. 17
110 Widtsoe, *Evidences and Reconciliations*, p. 195.
111 *Articles of Faith*, pp. 474-75. This follows logically from Mormon teaching about the fall. Why should Adam's "sin" be imputed to us if it was not really a sin in the first place?

the following truth was made clear to him: "And I also beheld that all children who die before they arrive at the years of accountability, are saved in the celestial kingdom of heaven."[112] Joseph Fielding Smith explains that the age of accountability has been set by the Lord at eight years, referring to *Doctrine and Covenants* 68:27 for proof.[113]

Mormons admit that Christ was the only person who ever lived without sin.[114] Since the pre-existent spirits of men are held to have been sinless in the beginning, and since children are considered to be without sin until they reach the age of eight, one wonders where the universal tendency to sin comes from. It would seem that the only explanation left is the common Pelagian one: imitation of other sinners. It is certainly clear that Mormons deny both original guilt and original pollution; they are thus completely Pelagian with respect to the doctrine of original sin.

Free Agency. One of the most prominent aspects of the Mormon doctrine of man is the insistence that man is a free agent: that is, that man does not act out of compulsion, but that every man is free to act for himself. This teaching is repeatedly stated in the Mormon scriptures: "I . . . have given unto the children of men to be agents unto themselves" (*Doctrine and Covenants* 104:17). Free agency is ascribed by Mormons to God, to pre-existent spirits, and to man:

> Agency is the ability and freedom to choose good or evil. It is an eternal principle which has existed with God from all eternity. The spirit offspring of the Father had agency in pre-existence and were thereby empowered to follow Christ or Lucifer according to their choice. It is by virtue of the exercise of agency in this life that men are enabled to undergo the testing which is an essential part of mortality.[115]

The great sin of Satan was that he tried to take away man's free agency. The Book of Moses pictures Satan as coming before God in the beginning and saying: "Behold, here am I, send me, I will be thy son, and I will redeem all mankind, that one soul shall not be lost . . . wherefore give me thine honor" (4:1). The third verse of this chapter thus describes Satan's pernicious error: "Wherefore, because that Satan rebelled against me, and sought

[112] *Teachings of the Prophet Joseph Smith*, p. 107.
[113] *Doctrines of Salvation*, II, 53.
[114] McConkie, *op. cit.*, p. 665.
[115] *Ibid.*, p. 25.

to destroy the agency of man, which I, the Lord God, had given him, . . . I caused that he should be cast down. . . ."

Free agency is therefore "an essential part of the great plan of redemption."[116] "It [free agency] is the only principle upon which exaltation can come. It is the only principle upon which rewards can be given in righteousness."[117]

In the light of what was said about the fall, it is clear that Mormons do not admit that man lost his ability to choose and to do the good through the fall. He is still able at every moment to make the right choices or to repent of whatever wrong choices he may have made. Here again the basically Pelagian nature of Mormon theology becomes evident.

DOCTRINE OF CHRIST

THE PERSON OF CHRIST

The Pre-existence of Christ. Mormons, as we have seen, identify Christ with Jehovah. Jehovah existed prior to his incarnation as the "first-born" of the myriads of pre-existent spirits. The following statements from James Talmage, in his *Articles of Faith,* make this clear: "Among the spirit-children of Elohim the firstborn was and is Jehovah or Jesus Christ to whom all others are juniors" (p. 471). "Jesus Christ is not the Father of the spirits who have taken or yet shall take bodies upon this earth, for He is one of them. He is The Son as they are sons or daughters of Elohim" (pp. 472-73). Note also the following statements from *Doctrine and Covenants*:

> And now, verily I say unto you, I was in the beginning with the Father, and am the First-born;
> And all those who are begotten through me are partakers of the glory of the same, and are the church of the First-born.
> Ye were also in the beginning with the Father. . . (93:21-23).

From these statements it is evident that, for Mormons, the only difference between Christ and us is that Christ was the first-born of Elohim's children, whereas we, in our pre-existence, were "born" later. The distinction between Christ and us is therefore one of degree, not one of kind.

If the devil and the demons were also spirit-children of Elohim, it must follow that they, too, are Jesus' brothers. This is exactly

---

[116] *Ibid.,* p. 25.
[117] Smith, *Doctrines of Salvation,* I, 70.

what one Mormon writer says: "As for the Devil and his fellow spirits, they are brothers to man and also to Jesus and sons and daughters of God in the same sense that we are."[118]   One could therefore even say that, for Mormons, the difference between Christ and the devil is not one of kind, but of degree!

The Divinity of Christ. From the foregoing it has already become evident that in Mormon theology Jesus Christ is basically not any more divine than any one of us.   We have previously noted that Mormons deny the Holy Trinity: Father, Son, and Holy Spirit, so they teach, are not one God but three gods.   It remains further to note that Christ is not considered equal to the Father: "Jesus is greater than the Holy Spirit, which is subject unto him, but his Father is greater than he."[119]   Though it is said that Christ "created" this earth under the Father's direction, it is also said that certain pre-existent spirits, like Adam and Joseph Smith, helped him.   Further confirming Mormonism's denial of the essential deity of Christ is the following statement by Mormon elder B. H. Roberts:

> The divinity of Jesus is the truth which now requires to be reperceived . . . the divinity of Jesus and [the divinity] of all other noble and saintly souls, insofar as they, too, have been inflamed by a spark of Deity — insofar as they, too, can be recognized as manifestations of the Divine.[120]

When we recall that the goal of Mormon eschatology is for man to attain godhood,[121] we conclude that the Christ of Mormonism is a far cry from the Christ of the Scriptures.   Neither his divinity nor his incarnation are unique.   His divinity is not unique, for it is the same as that to which man may attain.   His incarnation is not unique, for it is no different from that of other gods before him, who were incarnated on other earths; nor is it different from that of man, who also was a pre-existent spirit before he was incarnated on this earth.

The Virgin Birth of Christ. One finds occasional references in Mormon writings to the Virgin Mary.   One wonders, however, whether Mormons are entitled to use this term, since they insist

---

[118] John Henry Evans, *An American Prophet* (New York: Macmillan, 1933), p. 241.

[119] Joseph Fielding Smith, *Doctrines of Salvation*, I, 18.

[120] *Teachings of the Prophet Joseph Smith;* p. 347, last paragraph of n. 3.

[121] McConkie, *op. cit.*, p. 294.

that the body of Jesus Christ was literally begotten, though they
grant that he was conceived by Mary. When the question is asked,
By whom was this body begotten? Mormons are put "on the spot."
There exists a rather embarrassing statement by Brigham Young
which seems to give the impression that the body of Jesus Christ
was begotten by Adam (who presumably possessed some kind of
body at the time):

> When the Virgin Mary conceived the child Jesus, the Father
> had begotten him in his own likeness. . . . And who is the
> Father? He is the first of the human family; and when he
> [Christ] took a tabernacle, it was begotten by his Father in
> heaven, after the same manner as the tabernacles of Cain, Abel,
> and the rest of the sons and daughters of Adam and Eve. . . .
>
> Jesus, our elder brother, was begotten in the flesh by the
> same character that was in the Garden of Eden, and who is
> our Father in Heaven. . . .[122]

The statements: "the first of the human family," "after the same
manner as the tabernacles of Cain, Abel, and the rest of the sons
and daughters of Adam and Eve," and "the same character that
was in the Garden of Eden," certainly give the casual reader the
impression that President Young intended to say that the body of
Jesus was begotten by Adam.

Joseph Fielding Smith, however, goes into this question at great
length, insisting that Brigham Young did not mean to teach that
the body of Christ was begotten by Adam. He bends over back-
wards in his attempt to prove that Young really meant to say that
the body of Christ was begotten by our heavenly Father who is
distinct from Adam.[123] On another page Smith expresses himself
very plainly:

> Our Father in Heaven is the Father of Jesus Christ, both in
> the spirit and in the flesh. . . . I believe firmly that Jesus Christ
> is the Only-Begotten Son of God in the flesh. . . . Christ was
> begotten of God. He was not born without the aid of Man, and
> that Man was God.[124]

Talmage, in his *Articles of Faith,* expresses the same opinion:
". . . Elohim is literally the Father of the spirit of Jesus Christ
and also of the body in which Jesus Christ performed his mission
in the flesh. . ." (p. 466). ". . . He [Christ] is essentially greater

---

[122] *Journal of Discourses,* I, 50-51; quoted in Smith, *Doctrines of
Salvation,* I, 102.
[123] *Doctrines of Salvation,* I, 101-106.
[124] *Ibid.,* p. 18.

than any and all others, by reason . . . of His unique status in the flesh as the offspring of a mortal mother and of an immortal, or resurrected and glorified, Father" (p. 472).

It is difficult for non-Mormons to grasp at first reading what is being said here, since we are not accustomed to thinking of God the Father as having a physical body. What these men are saying is that, according to Mormon theology, the body of Jesus Christ was the product of the physical union of God the Father and the Virgin Mary. One shudders to think of the revolting implications of this view, which brings into what is supposed to be "Christian" theology one of the most unsavory features of ancient pagan mythology! The reader may judge for himself whether Mormons are still entitled to say that they believe in "the Virgin birth."[125]

Christ's Polygamous Marriage. According to Mormon doctrine, Jesus Christ was no more essentially divine before his incarnation than any of us. As we shall see when we discuss the Mormon doctrine of salvation, "there can be no exaltation to the fulness of the blessings of the celestial kingdom outside of the marriage relation."[126] Couples whose marriages have not been sealed for eternity become angels and not gods in the life to come; only those sealed to each other for eternity become gods (*Doctrine and Covenants* 132:19, 20). This would imply that if Jesus Christ was not married during his earthly life, he could not rise higher than an angel in the next life.[127]

We are therefore not surprised to find the following statements attributed to one of the members of the first Council of Twelve Apostles, Orson Hyde:

> If at the marriage of Cana of Galilee, Jesus was the bridegroom and took unto him Mary, Martha and the other Mary, it shocks not our nerves. If there was not attachment and familiarity between our Saviour and these women, highly proper only in the relation of husband and wife, then we have no sense of propriety.[128]
>
> We say it was Jesus Christ who was married whereby He

---

[125] One may well question whether Joseph Fielding Smith's interpretation of Brigham Young's remark really conveys what Young intended to say. Be that as it may, Smith's substitute explanation of the birth of Jesus Christ is no more acceptable to a Bible-believing Christian than is the conception attributed to Young which Smith has attempted to refute.

[126] Smith, *Doctrines of Salvation,* II, 65.

[127] Gordon H. Fraser, *Is Mormonism Christian?* (Chicago: *Moody Press,* 1957), p. 61.

[128] *Journal of Discourses,* II, 81-82; quoted in Fraser, *op. cit.,* p. 62.

could see His seed before He was crucified. I shall say here that before the Saviour died He looked upon His own natural children as we look upon ours. When Mary came to the sepulchre she saw two angels and she said unto them "they have taken away my Lord or husband."[129]

THE WORK OF CHRIST

The Atonement. According to Mormon theology, Adam's fall demanded an atonement; such an atonement was necessary to satisfy divine justice. "He had offered Himself, in the primeval council in heaven, as the subject of the atoning sacrifice made necessary by the foreseen transgression of the first man. . . ."[130] Hence Christ came to earth to make this atonement. This atonement was completely voluntary on Christ's part, and consisted particularly in His death by crucifixion. Talmage speaks of "the vicarious nature of his death as a foreordained and voluntary sacrifice, intended for and efficacious as a propitiation for the sins of mankind, thus becoming the means whereby salvation may be secured."[131]

We have observed, however, that for Mormons Adam's transgression was really a wise decision, and the fall was actually a blessing in disguise (above, pp. 53-54). When we are now told that the fall required an atonement, we are inclined to ask, Why? Mormons answer as follows: One of the results of the fall was that it brought physical death into the world; Christ's atonement was therefore necessary to deliver us all from death by providing for us all the right to be raised from the dead. A second result of the fall, however, was the introduction of spiritual death:

> Wherefore, I, the Lord God, caused that he [Adam] should be cast out from the Garden of Eden, from my presence, because of his transgression, wherein he became spiritually dead, which is the first death, even that same death which is the last death, which is spiritual, which shall be pronounced upon the wicked when I shall say: Depart, ye cursed (*Doctrine and Covenants* 29:41).

---

[129] *Journal of Discourses,* IV, 210; quoted in Fraser, *op. cit.,* p. 63. It should be added that we do not find this alleged marriage of Christ mentioned in the Mormon sacred books, or alluded to in Mormon doctrinal studies.

[130] Talmage, *Articles of Faith,* p. 79.

[131] *Ibid.,* p. 74. Cf. Chap. 4 in its entirety.

The atonement was necessary also in order to deliver us from this spiritual death.[132]

Mormons, accordingly, distinguish two main effects of the atonement: *general salvation* and *individual salvation*. *General salvation* is salvation from death through resurrection; this comes to everyone. Joseph Fielding Smith, who also uses the expression *unconditional redemption* to designate this, gives the following explanation of it:

> We need a little more explanation as to just what we mean by unconditional redemption. That means to restore us from this mortal state to the immortal state; in other words, to give unto us the resurrection. That comes to every creature, not only to men but also to the fish, the fowls of the air, and the beasts of the field. . . . All of them had spiritual existence before they were placed upon the earth; therefore they are to be redeemed.[133]

No condition needs to be fulfilled for man to receive salvation in this sense — this is a gift forced upon all mankind, which no one can reject.[134]

The second effect of the atonement is *individual salvation* (or, in Joseph Fielding Smith's words, *conditional redemption*). What salvation in this sense means will become evident as we discuss Mormon soteriology and eschatology; let it suffice here to say that it means escape from hell and entrance into one of the three Mormon heavens. *Individual salvation* will be given only to those who believe and obey. Certain classes, however, are excused from these requirements: children who die before the age of eight, and those "who have died not knowing the will of God concerning them, or who have ignorantly sinned" (Mosiah 3:11).

The Extent of the Atonement. The answer to the question about

---

[132] Note at this point a glaring inconsistency in Mormon doctrine. On the one hand it is said that the fall was a blessing in disguise, that Adam acted wisely, that his transgression was in accordance with law, and that the fall was necessary in order to enable man to propagate the race, so that myriads of pre-existent spirits could obtain mortal tabernacles and advance to exaltation. But now we are told that the fall was so calamitous an occurrence that it inflicted spiritual death with its consequent curse upon man. Apparently Mormons wish both to overthrow and to retain traditional theological thinking about the fall, as suits their purpose.

[133] *Doctrines of Salvation,* II, 10-11.

[134] Note that at this point the crucial principle of free agency is surrendered.

the extent of the atonement depends on which effect of the atonement is being contemplated. If one is thinking of *general salvation,* as defined above, the extent of the atonement is absolutely universal. There will be a resurrection for everyone, including even the animals. If one is thinking of *individual salvation,* however, certain qualifications must be made. Talmage expresses himself on this point as follows:

> But besides this universal application of the atonement, whereby all men are redeemed from the effects of Adam's transgression both with respect to the death of the body and inherited sin, there is application of the same great sacrifice as a means of propitiation for individual sins through the faith and good works of the sinner.
>
> The individual Effect of the Atonement makes it possible for any and every soul to obtain absolution from the effect of personal sins, through the mediation of Christ; but such saving intercession is to be invoked by individual effort as manifested through faith, repentance, and continued works of righteousness.[135]

Since, for Mormons, not all will attain individual salvation, the effect of the atonement in this sense is not universal. In this sense the atonement, though intended for all, is efficacious only for those who believe and obey.

Mormons often claim to believe that Christ died to save everybody. When this claim is made, the non-Mormon must first determine in what sense the word *save* is here used. If it is used as meaning *general salvation,* all it means to say is that Christ died so that everyone may be raised from the dead. According to Mormon teachings, however, as we shall see more clearly under the next doctrinal heading, Christ's atonement does not determine where man will go after the resurrection, since this is determined by man's own actions. Mormon theology thus leaves us with a Christ who does not really save in the full, Biblical sense of this word, but only gives man an opportunity to save himself from hell.

There is another way in which Mormons limit Christ's power to save. Joseph Fielding Smith writes:

> Joseph Smith taught that there were certain sins so grievous that man may commit, that they will place the transgressors beyond the power of the atonement of Christ. If these offenses are committed, then the blood of Christ will not cleanse them

[135] *Articles of Faith,* pp. 86-87, 89.

from their sins even though they repent.   Therefore their
only hope is to have their own blood shed to atone, as far as
possible, in their behalf.

> . . . Man may commit certain grievous sins — according to his
light and knowledge — that will place him beyond the reach of
the atoning blood of Christ.   If then he would be saved he
must make sacrifice of his own life to atone — so far as in
his power lies — for that sin, for the blood of Christ alone
under certain circumstances will not avail.[136]

In the case of grievous sins, therefore, man must add his own blood
to the blood of Christ to atone for his transgression.   One wonders
who is to determine when a sin has become so heinous as to re-
quire this kind of "blood atonement."   What deficiency in the
sacrifice of Christ makes it inadequate to atone for such sins?

DOCTRINE OF SALVATION

Individual Salvation.   We have already noted the distinctions
Mormons make between general and individual salvation.   How,
now, does one receive individual salvation?   Mormons vigorously
reject the doctrine of justification by faith.   James Talmage, in
fact, calls this a "pernicious doctrine," and states, "The sectarian
dogma of justification by faith alone has exercised an influence
for evil."[137]   Articles 3 and 4 of the Articles of Faith read as
follows:

> 3. We believe that through the Atonement of Christ, all man-
kind may be saved, by obedience to the laws and ordinances of
the Gospel.
> 4. We believe that the first principles and ordinances of the
Gospel are: first, Faith in the Lord Jesus Christ; second, Repentance; third, Baptism by immersion for the remission of sins;
fourth, Laying on of hands for the gift of the Holy Ghost.

Putting these two articles together, it appears that, in Mormonism, one is saved by faith plus works, with emphasis on the works.
Mormons insist that one must have faith in the Lord Jesus Christ;
it must not be forgotten, however, that faith in Christ and faith
in Joseph Smith must go together.[138]   Very revealing, in fact, is
the following statement from *Doctrine and Covenants*: "Joseph
Smith, the Prophet and Seer of the Lord, has done more, save

[136] *Doctrines of Salvation,* I, 135, 134.
[137] *Articles of Faith,* p. 479.
[138] Smith, *Doctrines of Salvation,* II, 302-3.

Jesus only, for the salvation of men in this world, than any other man that ever lived in it" (135:3).

The main emphasis in Mormon soteriology, however, is on works. Because of the general effect of Christ's atonement, every man shall receive immortality — that is, shall be raised from the dead. Not every man, however, shall receive salvation in the individual sense — that is, shall go to one of the three Mormon heavens. Salvation in this sense depends on one's merits:

> Salvation is twofold: General — that which comes to all men irrespective of a belief (in this life) in Christ — and, Individual — that which man merits through his own acts through life and by obedience to the laws and ordinances of the gospel.[139]

Mormons distinguish various degrees of salvation. The highest is sometimes called *eternal life* and sometimes *exaltation*. To gain eternal life means to partake of the same life which the Father possesses. Receiving exaltation means to become like God — or, in blunter, but more accurate language, to become a god. To become eligible for this highest degree of salvation, however, one must obey all the commandments of God:

> Very gladly would the Lord give to every one eternal life, but since that blessing can come only on merit — through the faithful performance of duty — only those who are worthy shall receive it.
>
> . . . To be exalted one must keep the whole law.
>
> . . . To receive the exaltation of the righteous, in other words [,] eternal life, the commandments of the Lord must be kept in all things.[140]

It has apparently never occurred to Mr. Smith that no one can "keep the commandments of the Lord in all things." Does not the Apostle John say, "If we say that we have no sin, we deceive ourselves, and the truth is not in us" (I John 1:8)?

Celestial Marriage. A very important point to remember in this connection, however, is that to receive the fullness of exaltation a man must have a wife and a woman must have a husband. Complete fulfillment of the commandments of God requires that a couple must be sealed to each other for both time and eternity in a temple ceremony.[141] This leads to a consideration of the doctrine of celestial marriage — one of the key doctrines of Mormonism. By way of background we should note what is said in

[139] *Ibid.,* I, 134.
[140] *Ibid.,* II, 5, 6.
[141] *Ibid.,* II, 43-44.

Section 132 of *Doctrine and Covenants.* In verses 15 and 16 of this section we read that, if a man should marry a wife not by the word of the Lord, this marriage will not be in force when the parties have died; hence, when these parties have left the present world, they are not gods but only angels in heaven, destined to minister everlastingly to those who are more worthy than they. Verses 19 and 20 go on to state that if, however, a man shall marry a wife by the word of the Lord, and this marriage is sealed to them by him who is anointed, this marriage shall be of full force when the parties are out of this world; they shall receive glory, "which glory shall be a fulness and a continuation of the seeds forever and ever. Then shall they be gods, because they have no end. . . ."

This implies that, for Mormons, there are two kinds of marriage: marriage for time, and marriage for eternity (or celestial marriage). A marriage for time — one that is not performed in a temple — will be dissolved by death. People so married will be single in the life to come, and will there live as angels, not as gods; their children will be left without parents in the future life, unless they are adopted by parents who have been sealed for eternity. Those, however, who have been married in a temple have been sealed to each other for eternity; their union will last forever. Parents who have been so sealed to each other "will have eternal claim upon their posterity, and will have the gift of eternal increase, if they obtain the exaltation. . . . All who obtain this exaltation will have the privilege of completing the full measure of their existence and they will have a posterity that will be as innumerable as the stars of heaven."[142] Children born to such parents while the latter are in the state of exaltation, Smith says on another page, will be spirit children, not clothed upon with tabernacles of flesh and bones.[143] In the light of all this, it is therefore not surprising to find Bruce McConkie saying:

> The most important single thing that any member of the Church of Jesus Christ of Latter-day Saints can ever do in this world is to marry the right person by the right authority in the right place.[144]

It would appear from the above that no one can receive complete

[142] *Ibid.,* II, 44.
[143] *Ibid.,* II, 68.
[144] *Mormon Doctrine,* p. 111. Note that celestial marriage thus appears to be more important to Mormons than faith in Jesus Christ.

fullness of salvation, including the attainment of the status of god-hood, unless he or she has been married to someone by means of a temple ceremony. Exceptions to this rule are, however, allowed for. Realizing that the woman does not usually take the initiative in a marriage proposal, Joseph Fielding Smith states that if a woman has remained single against her wishes, but would be per-fectly willing to obey the ordinance of celestial marriage if an opportunity should present itself, no blessing shall be withheld from her — in other words, she can still attain to the state of exaltation.[145] The same author mentions another exception: a faithful Mormon wife whose husband shows no interest in the Mormon Church will be given to another husband in the life to come, and will thus receive all the blessings of the celestial king-dom.[146]

It is quite clear, therefore, that Mormons have substituted for the Biblical doctrine of salvation by grace alone the unscriptural teaching of salvation by works.

DOCTRINE OF THE CHURCH AND SACRAMENTS

DOCTRINE OF THE CHURCH

Mormons teach that the Church of Jesus Christ was in a state of apostasy until the Mormon Church was founded in 1830. This apostasy began already in the early centuries of the Christian era and was not rectified even by the Reformation, since the Reformers had no direct revelations from heaven. The Lord, however, re-established His church in the last days through the Prophet Joseph Smith who, together with Oliver Cowdery, received both the Aaronic and the Melchizedek priesthood. This event Mormons designate as "the Restoration of the Church"; hence they call their own organization, "The Restored Church." James Talmage gives expression to Mormon convictions about the church when he says:

> The Latter-day Saints declare their high claim to be the true church organization, similar in all essentials to the organiza-tion effected by Christ among the Jews. This people of the last days profess to have the Priesthood of the Almighty, the

---

[145] *Doctrines of Salvation*, II, 76.
[146] *Answers to Gospel Questions*, III, 24. It is important to note in this connection that the *Book of Mormon*, which is supposed to contain "the fulness of the everlasting Gospel" (see above, p. 10), says nothing whatever about the doctrine of celestial marriage.

power to act in the name of God, which power commands respect both on earth and in heaven.[147]

The Mormon Church claims to be the only true church because it is, so it contends, the only church since the time of Christ which has received divine revelation (through Joseph Smith and others), and which may still continue to receive divine revelation through its presidents. Joseph Smith himself was once asked, "Will everybody be damned, but Mormons?" His answer was, "Yes, and a great portion of them, unless they repent, and work righteousness."[148] In the same vein, Brigham Young once said, ". . . Every spirit that does not confess that God has sent Joseph Smith, and revealed the everlasting gospel to and through him, is of Antichrist. . . ."[149] Orson Pratt, one of the early apostles of the Mormon Church, asserted that it is bold impudence for the non-Mormon churches to call themselves Christian churches, since

> They have nothing to do with Christ, neither has Christ anything to do with them, only to pour out upon them the plagues written. . . . All who will not now repent, as the authority is once more restored to the earth, and come forth out of the corrupt apostate churches and be adopted into the Church of Christ and earnestly seek after the blessings and miraculous gifts of the gospel shall be thrust down to hell, saith the Lord God of Hosts.[150]

These quotations speak for themselves. Mormons claim that they are the only group of God's true people on earth, and that those not in this group must enter it, either while still living or after they have died, in order to be saved.[151] In common with all cults, Latter-day Saints repudiate the Biblical truth of the universality of the church: the doctrine that the true church of Jesus Christ is not to be identified exclusively with any one earthly organization, but that it includes members of various denominations scattered throughout the earth. By relegating all of present-day and most of past Christendom to the status of apostasy, Mormonism reveals its utterly anti-Scriptural sectarianism.

[147] *Articles of Faith*, p. 204.
[148] *Teachings of the Prophet Joseph Smith*, p. 119.
[149] *Discourses of Brigham Young*, p. 435.
[150] Series of Pamphlets, No. III, p. 8, and No. V, p. 8; quoted in Henry C. Sheldon, *A Fourfold Test of Mormonism* (New York: Abingdon Press, 1914), p. 99.
[151] "If it had not been for Joseph Smith and the restoration, there would be no salvation. There is no salvation outside The Church of Jesus Christ of Latter-day Saints" (McConkie, *Mormon Doctrine,* p. 603).

DOCTRINE OF THE SACRAMENTS

Baptism. Mormons teach that baptism is absolutely necessary for salvation; it is therefore one of the "ordinances of the Gospel" which must be obeyed if one would be saved (compare Article 4 of the Articles of Faith). Note the following statements from *Doctrine and Covenants*: ". . . Thou shalt declare repentance and faith on the Savior, and remission of sins by baptism. . ." (19:31). "Verily, verily, I [Christ] say unto you [Joseph Smith], they who believe not on your words, and are not baptized in water in my name, for the remission of their sins, that they may receive the Holy Ghost, shall be damned. . ." (84:74). It is clear that, for Mormons, one can obtain remission of sins only through baptism, which rite must have been preceded by repentance. If sins are committed after one has been baptized, the *law of forgiveness* requires the following: godly sorrow for sin, abandonment of sin, confession of sin, restitution for sin, and obedience to all law.[152]

In distinction from the Bible, the Mormon scriptures precisely define the mode of baptism: it is to be by immersion (3 Nephi 11:26; *Doctrine and Covenants* 20:74). As a matter of fact, one of the additions Joseph Smith made to the Book of Genesis in his revision of the Bible was the episode of Adam's baptism by immersion![153]

Infant baptism is opposed, since little children "are not capable of committing sin" (Moroni 8:8); hence they "need no repentance, neither baptism" (v. 11). In this chapter, supposedly a letter from Mormon to his son Moroni, the further statement is made: ". . . He that supposeth that little children need baptism is in the gall of bitterness and in the bonds of iniquity, for he hath neither faith, hope, nor charity; wherefore, should he be cut off while in the thought, he must go down to hell" (v. 14). It is further specified in *Doctrine and Covenants* 68:27 that children shall be baptized when they are eight years old.

Baptism for the Dead. This is one of the distinctive doctrines of the Mormon Church. Though the Book of Mormon, which is supposed to contain "the fulness of the everlasting Gospel," says nothing about this practice, Joseph Smith supposedly received revelations about this matter after the *Book of Mormon* had been "translated." The earliest of these revelations is said to have been received by Smith on January 19, 1841 (Section 124 of

[152] McConkie, *op. cit.*, pp. 271-73.
[153] Moses 6:51-68; cf. Inspired Version, Gen. 6:52-71.

Doctrine and Covenants); a later revelation occurred, it is alleged, in September of 1842 (Section 128). The substance of these "revelations" was as follows: Malachi 4:5 and 6 state that Elijah the Prophet will come before the great and dreadful day of the Lord, to turn the heart of the fathers to the children, and the heart of the children to their fathers. This passage is interpreted to mean that, unless there is a "welding link" of some kind or other between the fathers and the children, the earth will be smitten with a curse (*Doctrine and Covenants* 128:18).[154]

What is this "welding link"? It is baptism for the dead, spoken of by the Apostle Paul in I Corinthians 15:29. Since baptism is essential for salvation, and since many have died before the church was "restored" under Joseph Smith, it seems inevitable that most of the dead will be lost. However, the living may be baptized as substitutes for the dead — that is, for those who died without a knowledge of the restored gospel (128:5). The manner of this baptism is also by immersion, in a font which has been built beneath the surface of the ground to simulate the graves of the deceased (128:12 and 13). These baptisms must be performed in a temple (124:28-37), and must be carefully recorded; ideally there should be three witnesses present at every such baptism (128:3).

Baptism for the dead is an ordinance which was instituted from before the foundation of the world (124:33). This is a matter so important that the salvation of the living depends upon it: "for their [the ancestors'] salvation is necessary and essential to our salvation" (128:15). In fact, Joseph Smith said at one time: "Those saints who neglect it [baptism for the dead] in behalf of their deceased relatives, do it at the peril of their own salvation."[155] Very consistently, therefore, Joseph Fielding Smith denounces the

154 Mormons believe that the promise that Elijah would be sent to the earth before the dreadful day of the Lord would come was literally fulfilled. They insist that on April 3, 1836, in the Kirtland Temple, there appeared to Joseph Smith and Oliver Cowdery, in succession, Christ Himself, Moses, Elias, and Elijah. [Smith apparently did not realize that Elias was the Greek form of the Hebrew name Elijah.] Elijah explained that he was there in fulfillment of the prophecy of Malachi; and that he was committing "the keys of this dispensation" into the hands of Smith and Cowdery (*Doctrine and Covenants* 110). It is the bestowal of these keys, Mormons claim, which gives them the right and the authority to practice baptism for the dead.

155 *Teachings of the Prophet Joseph Smith,* p. 193.

Reorganized Church as an apostate church because it does not practice baptism for the dead.[156]

Mormons must, therefore, work for the salvation of the dead of their own lineage as far back as they can go.[157] If the dead accept the baptism performed for them, this baptism is credited to their account, just as if they had acted for themselves.[158] Not all the dead who are baptized by proxy will attain exaltation, however, but only those among them who are worthy of celestial glory, since salvation will be based on merit.[159] It should also be mentioned that, according to Mormon teaching, Christ will bring the Gospel to those in the spirit world who did not have an opportunity to hear it while they were on earth; these spirits may then repent of their sins and believe in Christ. Even though one then repents, however, he still cannot be saved unless someone has been baptized for him.[160]

It will be noted that this doctrine not only enhances the prestige of the Mormon Church as the only agency on earth through which men can be saved, but that it also enables Mormons to become, at least in part, "saviors" of their deceased relatives.

The Lord's Supper. Christ is said to have instituted the Lord's Supper among the Nephites (III Nephi 18:3). In administering the Lord's Supper, Mormons follow specific directions given in their sacred books (Moroni, Chapters 4 and 5; *Doctrine and Covenants* 20:76-79). They make one exception in following these directions, however; whereas the directions call for the use of wine, they use water instead. To support this practice they adduce *Doctrine and Covenants* 27:2, "For, behold, I say unto you, that it mattereth not what ye shall eat or what ye shall drink when ye partake of the sacrament. . . ." The words of explanation which introduce this section inform us that in August of 1830 Joseph Smith was on his way to purchase wine from some non-Mormons, since he did not have any at the moment. He was then met by a heavenly messenger, who gave him the revelation just quoted, adding that he must not purchase wine or strong drink from his enemies.

---

[156] *Doctrines of Salvation,* I, 265ff. See also the tract by the same author, "The 'Reorganized Church' vs. Salvation for the Dead" (Salt Lake City: Deseret News Press).
[157] *Doctrines of Salvation,* II, 167.
[158] *Ibid.,* II, 162.
[159] *Ibid.,* II, 185-86.
[160] *Ibid.,* II, 162, 182, 191.

This sacrament is administered weekly. All baptized members of the church in good standing, eight years old and older, must partake.[161] Warnings are sounded against partaking unworthily; such a partaking is said to bring damnation to the soul (3 Nephi 18:29).

Talmage explains that the Lord's Supper is not a means for securing the remission of sins, but is (1) a testimony of our faithfulness and our determination to keep God's commandments, and (2) a means whereby we receive "a continuing endowment of the Holy Spirit."[162]

DOCTRINE OF THE LAST THINGS

THE GATHERINGS

Article 10 of the Articles of Faith briefly sums up Mormon eschatology: "We believe in the literal gathering of Israel and in the restoration of the Ten Tribes; that Zion will be built upon this [the American] continent; that Christ will reign personally upon the earth; and, that the earth will be renewed and receive its paradisaical glory."

We shall consider first the so-called "gathering" doctrine referred to in the opening words of this article. Talmage explains that Mormons believe in the "severely literal fulfilment of prophecies relating to the dispersion of Israel."[163] Various Old Testament prophecies referring to the gathering of Israelites from captivity are literally interpreted by Mormons as pointing to a series of gatherings which shall occur before the Lord's return. In confirmation of this, they refer to the alleged appearance of Moses to Joseph Smith and Oliver Cowdery in the Kirtland Temple in 1836, at which time Moses committed to them "the keys of the gathering of Israel from the four parts of the earth, and the leading of the ten tribes from the land of the north" (*Doctrine and Covenants* 110:11). Though this gathering is to concern remnants of the nation of Israel, Gentiles are to have a part in it, and may thus share in the blessings of it.[164]

This gathering will involve three distinct phases:

(1) *The Gathering of Ephraim.* Ephraim, Joseph's younger son, it is said, received the birthright in Israel after Reuben, the

---

161 *Ibid.,* II, 348.
162 *Articles of Faith,* p. 175.
163 *Articles of Faith,* p. 336.
164 *Ibid.,* pp. 334-36.

oldest son of Jacob, had lost the birthright by his transgression.[165] The *Book of Mormon,* it is further claimed, came to Ephraim, since Joseph Smith was "a pure Ephraimite."[166] Ephraim, therefore, now holds the priesthood. Ephraim has received "the fulness of the everlasting gospel."[167] Ephraim must therefore be "gathered first to prepare the way, through the gospel and the priesthood, for the rest of the tribes of Israel when the time comes for them to be gathered to Zion."[168] Since most of the members of the Mormon Church today are said to be Ephraimites,[169] it is obvious that the gathering of Ephraim is going on at the present time. Ephraim is being gathered in America, to Zion, which was divinely designated as the gathering-place on the North American Continent.[170] Strictly speaking, Zion is the city of Independence, Missouri, within which a site for the temple was divinely revealed to Joseph Smith (*Doctrine and Covenants* 57:1-5). However, the divine purpose to make this city the gathering place for Ephraim is now being held in abeyance; hence Ephraim is being gathered today in the region of the Rocky Mountains. Zion, however, shall yet be established on the chosen site.[171]

(2) *The Gathering of the Jews.* Mormons distinguish between the Jews, who are descendants of the Kingdom of Judah, and the Israelites, who are descendants of the ancient Kingdom of Israel. A second phase of the "gathering" is that the Jews, as above defined, will be gathered in Palestine, in fulfillment of the predictions of the prophets. Mormons contend that the return of many Jews to Palestine in recent years indicates that this prophecy is now being fulfilled. The center of this gathering is the city of Jerusalem, which will be rebuilt before Christ returns. Most of the Jews who are being gathered to Jerusalem, however, will not receive Christ as their Redeemer until He manifests Himself to

---

[165] Smith, *Doctrines of Salvation,* III, 250-51.
[166] *Ibid.,* III, 253. This claim is made despite the fact that Smith was of English descent on his father's side and of Scotch descent on his mother's side! It might be noted here that Mormons understand the expression, "the stick of Ephraim," which occurs in Ezek. 37:16, as a Biblical designation of the *Book of Mormon.*
[167] *Ibid.,* III, 252.
[168] *Ibid.*
[169] *Ibid.* One wonders on what grounds Mormons base this assertion The implication of this is that not only the American Indians, as has been previously stated, but most members of the Mormon Church are actually Israelites!
[170] Talmage, *Articles of Faith,* p. 352.
[171] *Ibid.,* p. 353.

them in person.[172] After Christ has returned to earth, there will be two capitals over which He shall reign during the millennium: Zion (or Independence, Missouri) on the American Continent; and Jerusalem in Palestine.[173]

(3) *The Gathering of the Lost Ten Tribes.* There will be one more gathering before Christ returns, namely, that of the lost ten tribes of Israel. These tribes, it is believed, are still hidden somewhere "in the land of the north." Christ, it is said, went to minister to them after his visit to the Nephites.[174] Before Christ returns, these ten tribes will be regathered and will be led to Zion,[175] where they will receive the crowning blessings from those of Ephraim, the "first-born of Israel," who by this time will all have been gathered in Zion.[176]

When all these gatherings shall have been completed, Christ will return to earth to set up His millennial kingdom. Before the millennium. is discussed, however, something should be said about the return of the City of Enoch. In a section which Joseph Smith added to the Book of Genesis, reproduced in *The Pearl of Great Price* as the Book of Moses, we read that Enoch, a preacher of righteousness in the antediluvian world, built a city which was called the City of Holiness, or Zion (Moses 7:19). This city, in process of time, was taken up into heaven (v. 21; cf. v. 69). Verse 62 of this chapter describes the future gathering of the elect from the four quarters of the earth into a holy city, which shall be called "Zion, a New Jerusalem." In verse 63 we read, "And the Lord said unto Enoch: Then shalt thou and all thy city meet them there. . . ." Verse 64 indicates that after this has happened the earth shall rest for a thousand years. From this passage we gather that, according to Mormon teachings, this heavenly city will return to the earth just before the millennium (or, perhaps, shortly after the millennium has begun, as McConkie thinks).[177] Talmage is of the opinion that the New Jerusalem which the Apostle John sees descending out of heaven, according to Revelation 21:2, is actually the City of Enoch coming down to earth. He adds: ". . . The people or Zion of

---

[172] Smith, *Doctrines of Salvation,* III, 9.
[173] *Ibid.,* III, 69-70. Just how Christ, in His physical body, will be able to rule from both capitals simultaneously, we are not told.
[174] Talmage, *Articles of Faith,* p. 340.
[175] *Ibid.,* p. 341.
[176] Smith, *Doctrines of Salvation,* III, 252-3.
[177] *Mormon Doctrine,* p. 774.

Enoch and the modern Zion, or the gathered saints on the western continent, will become one people."[178]

THE MILLENNIUM

According to Article 10 of the Articles of Faith, Mormons believe that Christ will reign personally upon the earth. This reign will occur during the millennium. Mormons believe that there will be two resurrections: one at the beginning and one at the end of the millennium. At the beginning of the millennium the believing dead will be raised (*Doctrine and Covenants* 88:97, 98); these shall be caught up to meet the returning Lord in the air, and shall descend with Him. At this time the "saints that are upon the earth, who are alive, shall be quickened and be caught up to meet Him."[179] Among those who are raised at this time will be included the heathen who were groping for the light, but did not hear the Gospel (45:54). This resurrection Mormons call "the first resurrection."

As the millennium begins, all the wicked shall be "burned as stubble" (29:9); this does not mean annihilation, however, but sudden death. During the entire millennium the spirits of the wicked will remain in the prison-house of the spirit world. Here they will be able to repent and to cleanse themselves through the things they shall suffer.[180]

A great era of peace will now be ushered in. Satan will be bound, and his power will be restrained. There will be no enmity between man and beast; love will rule supreme.[181] Men will be mostly zealous in the service of their reigning Lord. Yet sin will not be wholly abolished, nor will death be banished.[182] All who continue to live during the millennium will reach the age of one hundred years, and will then suddenly be changed to immortality, and be "caught up" (*Doctrine and Covenants* 101:30, 31). Since resurrected saints are also living on the earth at this time, mortal and immortal people shall be living side by side.

The great work of the millennium will be temple work: baptism for the dead. During the millennium mortals will be able to be

---

[178] *Articles of Faith*, p. 352.
[179] *Doctrine and Covenants* 88:96. Apparently Joseph Smith did not realize that the word "quicken" means "to make alive"! Why should those already alive still have to be "quickened"?
[180] Smith, *Doctrines of Salvation*, III, 59-60.
[181] Talmage, *Articles of Faith*, p. 369.
[182] *Ibid.*, p. 371.

baptized for all those who have lived from the beginning of time. Mortals will be directed in this work by the resurrected saints and the Saviour.[183]

Though the wicked are no longer on the earth, many non-Mormons who have lived "clean lives" and were therefore not put to death when Christ returned will also be among those who enjoy the millennium. During the millennium the Gospel must be preached to them "until all men are either converted or pass away."[184]

At the end of the millennium all the wicked will be raised.[185] This will be the second resurrection. Also at this time Satan will be loosed and will again assert his power; some of those living on the earth will follow Satan in his last attempt to deceive the nations, and will thus become Sons of Perdition. The hosts whom Satan will gather will include some from the inhabitants of the earth, and some from among the wicked dead who have just been raised. A last great battle will be fought, in which Satan and his hosts will be defeated.[186]

THE FINAL STATE

At the end of the millennium the earth will be dissolved. It shall then be renewed, or "raised with a resurrection," thus becoming "a celestial body, so that they of the celestial order may possess it forever and ever."[187] According to Talmage the earth will then become "a celestialized body fit for the abode of the most exalted intelligences."[188] It will then no longer be opaque, as at present, but, like the sun and the other stars, full of light and glory. In fact, all the great stars that we see, including our sun, are celestial worlds — worlds that have passed on to their exaltation.[189]

---

[183] Smith, *Doctrines of Salvation*, III, 58-59. A Genealogical Society, with headquarters in Salt Lake City, is gathering genealogical statistics in order to prepare for this millennial temple work. According to the Statistical Report found in the April 13, 1963, issue of the *Church News,* genealogical records microfilmed in 13 countries during the year 1962 were equivalent to 154,174 printed volumes of approximately 300 pages per volume!

[184] *Ibid.,* I, 86.

[185] Talmage, *Articles of Faith,* p. 390.

[186] Smith, *Doctrines of Salvation,* I, 87.

[187] *Ibid.,* I, 87-88.

[188] *Articles of Faith,* p. 375.

[189] Smith, *Doctrines of Salvation,* I, 88-89.

What will be the final state of man? We should first note that, after the renewal of the earth, death will be completely banished.[190] There will, however, be quite a difference in the final state of various types of beings. Section 76 of *Doctrine and Covenants* is an important source of Mormon teachings on the final state. The heading prefacing this section states that before this vision came, Joseph Smith and Sidney Rigdon had concluded from various previous revelations that heaven must include more king-doms than one.

Mormon theology assigns beings in the final state to four different groups. The first of these groups consists of the so-called *Sons of Perdition*. These are again divided into two classes: (a) The devil and his angels. The devil (Lucifer, a brother of Christ) rebelled against God (Elohim) in the pre-existent state, and enticed one-third of the spirits to follow him in his rebellion. In punishment for this rebellion, these spirits remain without bodies eternally,[191] and are denied redemption through Christ, since they have lost the power of repentance.[192] (b) Human beings whose sins have also placed them beyond "the present possibility of repentance and salvation."[193] These are people who "have known the power of God in this mortal life and then, having full knowledge of the power and purposes of God, rebel against Him, putting Jesus Christ to open shame."[194] Their transgres-sion is also described as the unpardonable sin, or as the blasphemy against the Holy Spirit.[195]

The Sons of Perdition, the human members of whom, according to one Mormon source, are "but a small portion of the human race,"[196] will be permanently consigned to hell. There they are "doomed to suffer the wrath of God, with the devil and his angels, in eternity"; for their sin "there is no forgiveness in this world nor in the world to come" (*Doctrine and Covenants* 76: 33, 34). Their torment will be endless, for "their worm dieth not and the fire is not quenched, which is their torment — and

---

190 Talmage, *Articles of Faith,* p. 378.
191 How does this harmonize with the Mormon view of the Holy Spirit, who is also said to be without a body?
192 Smith, *Doctrines of Salvation,* II, 219.
193 Talmage, *Articles of Faith,* p. 409.
194 Smith, *Doctrines of Salvation,* II, 219-20.
195 *Ibid.,* II, 221.
196 Smith and Sjodahl, *Doctrine and Covenants Commentary,* p. 453.

the end thereof, neither the place thereof, nor their torment, no man knows" (76:44, 45).[197]

The Sons of Perdition constitute the only group which shall not be redeemed (76:38). Those who are redeemed, however, will spend eternity in one of three different kingdoms, in each of which are to be found many gradations of glory. Beginning with the highest of these kingdoms, they are as follows:

(1) *The Celestial Kingdom.* This kingdom, which will be located on this earth after its renewal, "is prepared for the righteous, those who have been faithful in keeping the commandments of the Lord, and have been cleansed of all their sins."[198] Most of those who enter this kingdom (though not all) receive full exaltation; those who receive this exaltation constitute the "Church of the First-born" (*Doctrine and Covenants* 76:54); they are gods (76:58). They shall dwell in the presence of God and his Christ forever and ever (76:62). It will be remembered that those who reach this blessed state shall live with the spouses to whom they have been sealed for eternity, and with the children to whom they have been so sealed; they shall also continue to procreate children in the celestial state (though these shall be spirit children). It might be noted at this point that those who go into the Terrestrial and Telestial Kingdoms shall be denied the power of propagation, and shall live in "single blessedness," not as members of family groups.

(2) *The Terrestrial Kingdom.* This kingdom will be located on some sphere other than the earth, presumably another planet.[199] Into this kingdom the following will go:

1. Accountable persons who die without law. . .;
2. Those who reject the gospel in this life and who reverse their course and accept it in the spirit world;[200]

---

[197] That the Sons of Perdition shall suffer endlessly is also clearly taught by II Nephi 9:16. What puzzles non-Mormons, however, is the statement quoted above: "the end thereof . . . no man knows." It is possible to construe this sentence as meaning that nobody knows whether there will be an end, implying that there may be an end to their torment after all. Puzzling, too, is *Doctrine and Covenants* 19:10-12, where we are told that *endless punishment* is so called simply because it is the punishment of the Endless One. We are forced to conclude that there is some ambiguity in Mormon teaching on the question of eternal punishment.

[198] Joseph Fielding Smith, *Answers to Gospel Questions,* II, 208.

[199] *Ibid.,* II, 210.

[200] It will be noted that here Mormons adopt the unscriptural position that people who have rejected the gospel in this life will have another opportunity to accept it after death.

3. Honorable men of the earth who are blinded by the crafti-
ness of men and who therefore do not accept and live the gospel
law;

4. Members of the Church of Jesus Christ of Latter-day Saints
. . . who are not valiant, but who are instead lukewarm in their
devotion to the Church and to righteousness.[201]

Joseph Fielding Smith adds the comment that "all who enter
this kingdom must be of that class who have been morally clean."[202]
People in this kingdom will be ministered to by those in the
Celestial Kingdom (*Doctrine and Covenants* 76:87). They will
"receive of the presence of the Son, but not of the fulness of the
Father" (76:77).

(3) *The Telestial Kingdom.* This kingdom will be found on
still another earth.[203] "Into this kingdom will go all of those
who have been unclean in their lives. . . . These people who
enter there will be the unclean; the liars, sorcerers, adulterers, and
those who have broken their covenants."[204] These are people who
say they are of Paul, of Apollos, or of Cephas (*Doctrine and Covenants* 76:99.[205] They "receive not the gospel, neither the testimony
of Jesus, neither the prophets, neither the everlasting covenant"
(76:101). "These are they who are cast down to hell and suffer the
wrath of Almighty God until the fulness of times" (76:106). "Yet
these, after they have been punished for their sins and have been
turned over to the torments of Satan, shall eventually come forth,
after the Millennium, to receive the telestial kingdom."[206] These
people, in other words, will not be raised until the end of the
millennium. They will be quite numerous: their number will
be as great as the sand on the seashore (*Doctrine and Covenants*

[201] McConkie, *Mormon Doctrine,* p. 708. Reference is made to *Doctrine
and Covenants* 76:71-80.
[202] *Answers to Gospel Questions,* II, 209. One wonders what Smith
means by "morally clean." Is one who rejects the gospel in this life to be
considered "morally clean"?
[203] *Ibid.,* II, 210.
[204] *Ibid.,* II, 209.
[205] It should be noted here that if any group is guilty of the sin rebuked
by Paul in the passage here alluded to (I Cor. 1:12), it is the Mormons!
By placing a merely human leader, Joseph Smith, far higher than Paul or
Apollos or Cephas — almost as high as Jesus Christ, in fact — and by
accusing all those who belong to Christian churches of corruption, hy-
pocrisy, and apostasy (see *Pearl of Great Price,* p. 48, v. 19), Mormons
are doing precisely what the erring factions in Corinth were doing. Only
they are saying, "We are of Joseph."
[206] *Answers to Gospel Questions,* II, 209. See *Doctrine and Covenants*
88:100-101.

76:109). They shall be "judged according to their works, and every man shall receive . . . his own dominion, in the mansions which are prepared" (76:111). These "receive not of his [God's] fulness in the eternal world, but of the Holy Spirit, through the ministration of the terrestrial" (76:86). "They shall be servants of the Most High; but where God and Christ dwell they cannot come, worlds without end" (76:112).

Opportunity will be given for advancement within each of these three kingdoms. As regards the possibility of progression from one kingdom to another, Talmage declares that the scriptures make no positive affirmation.[207] On this point, however, Joseph Fielding Smith is much more dogmatic than Talmage: "It has been asked if it is possible for one who inherits the telestial glory to advance in time to the celestial glory. The answer to this question is, No!"[208]

Summarizing the above, we cannot in the strict sense of the term call the Mormons Universalists, since they do hold that some human beings (though their number is very small) will be consigned to everlasting punishment in hell, along with the devil and his angels. One could, however, call Mormons virtual Universalists since, according to their teaching, the vast majority of the human race will attain to some kind of salvation.

[207] *Articles of Faith*, p. 409.
[208] *Doctrines of Salvation*, II, 31.

IV. Appendix: The Book of Mormon

In the preceding discussion the question of the necessity for revelations additional to the Bible was touched upon. In this appendix we shall discuss the question of the genuineness of the *Book of Mormon* as an additional sacred scripture which purports to give additional revelation from God. We shall look at this matter from two points of view: the languages in which the plates basic to the *Book of Mormon* are said to have been written, and the transmission of the *Book of Mormon*.[1]

THE LANGUAGES OF THE BOOK OF MORMON

Mormons claim that the *Book of Mormon* is a book of divine revelation, given us by God in addition to the Bible. Let us see whether the facts concerning the alleged writing and transmission of the *Book of Mormon* bear out this claim. The Bible, as we know, was written in languages which were known and spoken by many: Hebrew, Aramaic, and Greek. The Old Testa-

---

[1] In the bibliography one will find a list of books dealing particularly with the *Book of Mormon*. To these may be added George B. Arbaugh's *Revelation in Mormonism*, E. D. Howe's *Mormonism Unveiled*, and Chapters 3 and 4 of James H. Snowden's *The Truth About Mormonism*. These volumes bring up such matters as contradictions between the *Book of Mormon* and the Bible, between the *Book of Mormon* and the other sacred books of Mormonism, and between the *Book of Mormon* and various statements by Joseph Smith; the so-called Spaulding-Rigdon theory of the origin of the *Book of Mormon;* and the relation between the *Book of Mormon* and archaeological discoveries on the American continent. Since these topics are adequately treated by other writers, this appendix will not touch upon them, but will deal with some aspects of the genuineness of the *Book of Mormon* which have not been fully dealt with elsewhere.

ment was written in the Hebrew language which was spoken in Palestine at the time when these writings were produced, with the exception of a few short sections in Aramaic (six chapters of the Book of Daniel and two passages in the Book of Ezra). The New Testament was written in Greek, which was at that time the common language of the Roman Empire and the literary language of Palestine. Although there was a time when the differences between the Greek of the New Testament and classical Greek led some scholars to presume that the former was a special kind of "Holy Ghost Greek," particularly devised by God for the purpose of communicating His revelation to man, the discovery during the last sixty years of thousands of extra-Biblical papyri dating from New Testament times, mostly commercial documents written in Greek, has proved that the Koine Greek of the New Testament was simply the everyday language which was in common use throughout the empire at that time.[2]

If, now, God intended to issue another set of sacred books, it would be expected that He would do so in another well-known language, the existence and character of which would be testified to by extra-canonical documents. Mormons claim, however, that the language in which the plates allegedly original to the *Book of Mormon* were written was "Reformed Egyptian" (Mormon 9:32); two verses later the following qualification is added: "But the Lord knoweth the things which we have written, and also that none other people knoweth our language; therefore he hath prepared means for the interpretation thereof." "Reformed Egyptian," therefore, is not a known language; neither do we possess documents or inscriptions of any sort which attest the existence of this language or help us understand its character. Is it likely that God would give us His newest and allegedly greatest Book of Scripture in a language completely unknown?

The force of this objection will be more fully realized as we reflect a bit further. The existence of manuscript copies of the books of the Bible in Hebrew, Aramaic, and Greek enables Bible scholars to study the Bible in these original languages. As anyone who has ever attempted to translate from one language to another knows, a translation is never a precise reproduction of the original text. Certain fine shades of meaning are invariably

---

[2] J. H. Moulton and G. Milligan, *The Vocabulary of the Greek Testament Illustrated by the Papyri* (Grand Rapids: Eerdmans, 1957), pp. xi-xii.

lost in translation, since one can never fully express in the second language everything that is expressed in the first language. Because we do have Biblical manuscripts in the original languages, however, Bible scholars (including ministers trained in Greek and Hebrew) can study the Bible in the original, and thus recapture the fine shades of meaning which the authors of the Bible (and, we should add, the Holy Spirit who inspired them) intended to convey. All this, however, is impossible in the case of the *Book of Mormon,* for there are no manuscript copies of the original documents from which this book was allegedly translated. Does it seem likely, now, that God would give us His latest sacred book in a manner so different from that in which He gave us the Bible? Why did God cause copies of Hebrew and Greek manuscripts of the books of the Bible to be preserved in greater number than those of any other ancient book, whereas in the case of the *Book of Mormon* He purportedly left with us only an English translation?

The existence of an extra-Biblical literature in the languages of the Bible constitutes a strong testimony to the genuineness of the Biblical writings. This type of testimony, however, is completely absent in the case of the *Book of Mormon,* since there exists no literature in "Reformed Egyptian." What assurance have we, then, that "Reformed Egyptian" was actually spoken and actually written? We must simply take one man's word for this: namely, that of Joseph Smith. Further, the existence of manuscripts in the original languages of the Bible and the existence of an extra-Biblical literature in these languages enable Biblical scholars to study the grammar of these languages and to engage in lexicographical studies. All of this type of study, however, is impossible in the case of "Reformed Egyptian." Why do we have no lexicons of "Reformed Egyptian," no grammars of "Reformed Egyptian," as we do have Hebrew lexicons and Hebrew grammars, Greek lexicons and Greek grammars? Does it seem likely that God went to all the trouble of having these additional revelations recorded in "Reformed Egyptian," only to allow all further traces of this language to disappear?

More should be said, however, about the "Reformed Egyptian" language. Nephi, who is alleged to have engraved the first "Reformed Egyptian" sacred plates, was a Jew who, it is said, lived originally in Jerusalem at about 600 B.C. At that time both the

spoken and written language of the Jews was Hebrew.[3]   It
would be expected, therefore, that Nephi, his brothers, and his
father, Lehi, would also speak and write in Hebrew.   However,
mirabile dictu, we find that Nephi, after having arrived in America, began to write on golden plates in "Reformed Egyptian!"
Not only so, but we find that the "Brass Plates of Laban" which
Lehi and his sons had taken with them were also written in
the Egyptian language!   As was mentioned, these brass plates
supposedly contained the five books of Moses, the genealogy of
Lehi, and "many of the prophecies from the beginning down to
and including part of those spoken by Jeremiah."[4]   Mosiah 1:4
tells us that the language of these plates was "the language of the
Egyptians."

We are to understand, then, that Nephi and his brothers found
in Jerusalem in the sixth century B.C. a set of brass plates containing large sections of the Hebrew Scriptures translated into
some form of Egyptian.   Leaving aside the question of the kind
of writing materials used (to which we shall return), we ask at
this time: Where did this Egyptian translation come from?   What
body of Egyptian scholars did this translating?   For what purpose
was this translation made?   If the Egyptian language was so
commonly used in Palestine at this time that an Egyptian translation of the Scriptures was required, why have we heard nothing
about this?   And why do we have no record of this Egyptian
translation — which, if it were to be found, would rival, if not
surpass, the Septuagint[5] in importance?

We now ask the further question: Where did Lehi and his
sons learn to read the Egyptian language so that they could
decipher these brass plates?   And where did Nephi learn the
Egyptian language well enough to write it on the golden plates?
In I Nephi 1:2 we hear Nephi saying, "Yea, I make a record in
the language of my father, which [the language?] consists of the
learning of the Jews and the language of the Egyptians."   But
where did Lehi learn "the language of the Egyptians"?   Were
not Lehi and his sons Hebrew-speaking Jews?   Mormon mis-

---

[3] For example: the Siloam Tunnel Inscription (7th century, B.C.) and
the Lachish Letters (early 6th century, B.C.) were written in Hebrew. Further, as is well known, Bible books written around this time, like Jeremiah,
Ezekiel, and Habakkuk, were written entirely in Hebrew.

[4] McConkie, *Mormon Doctrine,* p. 97; cf. Alma 37:3.

[5] The translation of the Old Testament into Greek, prepared in Alexan-
dria, Egypt, in the third and second centuries B.C.

sionaries have told the author that the reason Nephi and the Nephites wrote in Egyptian was that they were descendants of Joseph (who was the father of Manasseh), and that Joseph had lived in Egypt. True enough, but the entire nation of Israel had lived in Egypt for over 400 years; yet they did not speak and write Egyptian but Hebrew. Moses himself, who was trained in all the culture of the Egyptians, wrote not in Egyptian but in Hebrew. Why, then, should Nephi, who apparently had never lived in Egypt, write in Egyptian? Why should this small group of Jews from the tribe of Manasseh form a linguistic exception to the prevalence of Hebrew in Palestine?

One could counter, of course, that God could have caused them to learn Egyptian miraculously. But why this unnecessary miracle, when they already possessed a language, namely, Hebrew? And, further, since the plates were later to be miraculously translated into English by Joseph Smith, and were not to be left on earth, why, if there was to be a linguistic miracle, did not the Nephites learn to talk and write English? Then there would have been no need for a "translation."

This brings us to the further question of the character of this "Reformed Egyptian" language in which Nephi and subsequent Nephite scribes reportedly recorded the history of their nation. The official description of this language and of its characters is found in Mormon 9:32, "And now, behold, we have written this record according to our knowledge, in the characters which are called among us the reformed Egyptian, being handed down and altered by us, according to our manner of speech." So this was allegedly a somewhat altered form of an earlier pure Egyptian language, written in characters which had undergone a process of alteration. Unfortunately, we possess no samples of these characters; we can only surmise what type of script this is supposed to have been. One wishes that Moroni had specified whether the original Egyptian script which the Nephites had somewhat altered was hieroglyphic, hieratic, or demotic.[6] Whichever form it was, however, it seems reasonably sure that it was not an alphabetic script, since none of the three above-mentioned

---

[6] The three main types of Egyptian writing. Hieroglyphic began to be used about 3,000 B.C., and had passed out of use by 600 B.C. Hieratic was used alongside of hieroglyphic, and continued to be employed until the third century A.D. Demotic, a cursive derivative of hieratic, was used from about the 8th century B.C. to the 5th century A.D. See David Diringer, *The Alphabet* (New York: Philosophical Library, 1948), pp. 59, 64-67.

types of Egyptian are either syllabic or alphabetic.[7] This means that any of these types of Egyptian script would be extremely difficult to learn or to use, having a great number of characters picturing various objects and actions. This fact, plus the fact that in Egypt writing was not practiced by the common people but only by the priestly classes,[8] makes it all the more amazing that Lehi and his sons were able to read and write Egyptian.

This raises the question: Why did God choose to use this language and this script for His alleged latest book of revelation? Why, in other words, did God make Nephi and his descendants change from Hebrew to Egyptian? One can very easily understand why the change from Hebrew to Greek was made when the New Testament manuscripts were written: Greek was then the common language of the Greco-Roman world, the language in which the gospel would be able to command the widest hearing. There is a second reason: Greek is more highly inflected than Hebrew, having, for example, seven tenses instead of the two found in Hebrew, and thus providing opportunity for many additional shades of meaning. The language of the New Testament, therefore, is well adapted to convey the more advanced revelation about God and the plan of salvation which is given in the New Testament. But now the question begins to pinch: why the shift from Hebrew to Egyptian? The reason cannot be found in the suggestion that this was to be the language of the new land where they were going, since the land was at this time presumably uninhabited. As far as the Nephites themselves were concerned, what good reason would there be for their not continuing to talk and write in Hebrew, which they already knew and understood? Furthermore, neither can the reason be found in any possible superiority of the Egyptian language over the Hebrew as a mode of conveying divine revelation. For, as we have seen, all the types of Egyptian script were non-alphabetic, whereas Hebrew is a language written in alphabetic script. Does it seem likely, now, that God would, for His alleged final sacred book, shift from an alphabetically written language like Hebrew to a more primitive, non-alphabetically written language like Egyptian, which would be obviously less precise in conveying fine shades of meaning than either Hebrew or Greek? If, finally, Egyptian were a language in some respects superior to

[7] *Ibid.*, p. 67.
[8] *Ibid.*, p. 37.

Hebrew, and admirably suited to convey the new and final revelation, why did God permit all traces of this language to be lost and all these original documents to be removed from the earth? If God's intent from the beginning was to leave with us only an English translation of these documents, why could not this translation have been just as effectively made from Hebrew as from "Reformed Egyptian"?

The *Book of Mormon* raises another major linguistic problem, however. Moroni, as we have seen, supposedly completed his father Mormon's records, and added two books of his own, one of which was the Book of Ether. The latter was supposed to be an abridgment by Moroni of the twenty-four plates of Ether (Ether 1:2). Ether was a prophet of the Jaredites, and one of the last survivors of that race. The Jaredites, however, did not speak Egyptian; they "retained a tongue patterned after that of Adam."[9] The Book of Ether itself tells us that, at the time of the confusion of tongues at the tower of Babel, the language of the Jaredites was not confused, though all other languages were (1:33-37). Since Ether was a Jaredite, it seems reasonable to suppose that he wrote in the language of the Jaredites — a language which must have been utterly different from "Reformed Egyptian." Here is another amazing linguistic phenomenon: without supernatural help, such as was allegedly supplied to Joseph Smith when he did his work of translation, Moroni, whose language was "Reformed Egyptian," was able to decipher and abridge plates written in the language of the Jaredites, a language akin to that spoken by Adam and Eve!

Moroni, in fact, must have been quite a linguist. Apparently he knew Hebrew too. For note what he says, according to Mormon 9:33,

> And if our plates had been sufficiently large we should have written in Hebrew; but the Hebrew hath been altered by us also; and if we could have written in Hebrew, behold, ye would have had no imperfection in our record.

Talmage concludes from this statement that the Nephites continued to be able to read and write in Hebrew until the time of their extinction.[10] This was also a remarkable achievement! According to Talmage's comment, the Nephites remained bilingual for a period of a thousand years (from 600 B.C. to A.D. 421),

---

9 McConkie, *Mormon Doctrine*, p. 393.
10 *Articles of Faith*, p. 292.

able to read and write both in "Reformed Egyptian" and in Hebrew. They thus did far better than the Palestinian Jews, who
after the captivity generally no longer used Hebrew as the language of everyday life, but more and more used Aramaic instead.[11]
What a pity, further, that these Hebrew-reading Nephites did not
have a copy of the Old Testament Scriptures in the Hebrew, but
had to depend on an Egyptian translation on brass plates!

We are interested, now, in knowing why Moroni (and his father
Mormon) did not write the plates in Hebrew, which would, according to the last part of Mormon 9:33, have resulted in a more
perfect type of record. The reason given is that the plates were
not large enough. A strange reason indeed. Why did not Moroni
and Mormon simply write the Hebrew in smaller letters? Or why
did they not make larger plates? If the record would have been
more perfect in Hebrew, and if the Nephites could read Hebrew,
why did not these men exert every effort to convey the revelation
in the best possible medium?

When we attempt to reconstruct the scene, the reason given
seems more strange still. If one knew two languages and were
trying to decide in which of these two languages he should write
certain important material, does it seem likely that the crucial
factor in making this decision would be the size of the plates on
which he were writing? Would not the deciding factor rather be
the writer's greater competence in one language or the other? Or
if — as seems highly unlikely — one's competence would be equal
in both, would not the language chosen be the one which would
most effectively convey the material to be transmitted? According to Moroni's statement, that language would have been Hebrew. And yet Hebrew was not chosen. Does this seem likely?

Does it seem likely, further, that God would allow His revelation to be written in a language which would leave a somewhat
imperfect record simply because of a lack of room on the plates?
If it was important that the best possible record should be made —
and why shouldn't it be? — why did not God see to it that Mormon

---

[11] Frederic Kenyon, *Our Bible and the Ancient Manuscripts*, rev. by
A. W. Adams (N.Y.: Harper, 1958), p. 94. This Nephite linguistic
phenomenon is all the more remarkable when we reflect on the fact
that the Palestinian Jews largely lost their ability to use Hebrew during
their 70-year sojourn in Babylonian captivity, whereas the American
Nephites allegedly kept up their Hebrew during a 1000-year stay in a
foreign land, *while at the same time using "Reformed Egyptian" as their
main language!*

and Moroni were provided with a sufficient quantity of large plates?

THE TRANSMISSION OF THE BOOK OF MORMON

We concern ourselves next with the question of the transmission of the documents allegedly basic to the *Book of Mormon*. Here, too, we shall find a number of improbabilities. In the sixth century B.C. the most common forms of writing material in Palestine were papyrus and leather (or animal skin); the Hebrews also wrote on wood and potsherds. Rare examples of Mesopotamian clay-tablets with cuneiform writing have been found in Palestine, but these were obviously the work of foreigners.[12] The most common form in which books were made in those days was the roll, made of leather or papyrus, in which the various sheets were sewn or pasted together.[13] So common was this method of making books that the expression "roll of the book" (*megillath-see-pher*) is often used in the Bible to describe a book. Note particularly that this expression is used several times in the thirty-sixth chapter of the book of Jeremiah — a book written around the sixth century B.C. It is quite obvious, further, that the roll mentioned in Jeremiah 36 was not made of metal, since the king cut it into pieces with a penknife. It should, of course, be mentioned that writing on metal was not completely unknown, since a copper scroll has been discovered at Qumran. This scroll, however, was not a plate but a roll, and is dated much later than 600 B.C., being generally ascribed to the first century B.C.

In view of the above facts, does it seem likely that brass plates containing a large section of the Old Testament in Egyptian would be found in Palestine in 600 B.C.? We have previously discussed the problem of the language reputedly inscribed on these plates; the use of metal plates as writing material for an extensive document such as that described above, however, presents a problem as great as that of the language. The only other instance of writing on metal which is commonly known is the copper scroll of Qumran, as noted above; but even this was a roll, not a plate.[14]

---

[12] G. Ernest Wright, *Biblical Archaeology* (Philadelphia: Westminster Press, 1957), p. 197. Cf. Merrill F. Unger, *Archaeology and the Old Testament* (Grand Rapids: Zondervan, 1956), p. 275. Also Jack Finegan, *Light from the Ancient Past,* 2nd ed. (Princeton University Press, 1959), pp. 389-90.

[13] Wright, *op. cit.,* p. 197. Cf. Frederic Kenyon, *op. cit.,* pp. 37-38.

[14] It should be mentioned, however, that a bronze blade from the eleventh century B.C. has been found at Gebal or Byblos on the Mediter-

A similar question could be asked about the "golden plates" on which the Nephite records were made. Manuscripts from Central America and Mexico dating from pre-Columbian times were generally on coarse cloth or on paper.[15]   Great numbers of these pre-Columbian manuscripts are known to have been burned by fanatical Spanish priests — hence they could not have been made of metal.[16]   Does it seem likely, then, that the prehistoric inhabitants of the American continent would have kept their records on golden plates?

We have observed previously that no copies of the original plates from which Joseph Smith "translated" have been preserved; Mormons contend that Smith had to return these plates to the custody of Moroni.[17]   This brings us to the question of translation.   Joseph Smith, who had not been trained in "Reformed Egyptian," was nevertheless able to translate all these writings into English. Mormons claim, as we know, that Smith did this translating in a supernatural way, with the aid of the "Urim and Thummim."[18]   Here, already, as we have seen, there is great disparity between the Bible and the *Book of Mormon*.   In giving us the Bible, God gave us manuscripts in Hebrew and Greek which we can translate with the aid of lexicographical helps.   Does it seem likely that God would completely change His method and give us, in the instance of His later and reputedly superior revelation, only a translation but not the original language?   Does it seem likely that an untrained man can by looking through stones translate foreign characters?

We must next examine the nature of this alleged translation.

---

ranean coast, containing an inscription in Phoenician-Hebrew script.   Also. bronze arrowheads of the same period have been found near Bethlehem, each of them containing two words in the Phoenician-Hebrew script (*Views of the Biblical World,* International Publishing Co., 1960, II, 91). It should be noted, however, that these metal objects are a far cry from the type of "brass plates" described in the *Book of Mormon,* that the date of these objects is about five centuries before 600 B.C., and that the writing found on them is not Egyptian but a kind of early Hebrew. Note also that the blade was discovered at Byblos, which is some 160 miles north of Jerusalem, and that neither the blade nor the arrowheads present any kind of analogy for the writing of entire books on metal.

[15]   Diringer, *op. cit.,* p. 125.
[16]   *Ibid.*
[17]   McConkie, *op. cit.,* p. 300.
[18]   See above, p. 10 and n. 4 on that page.

It will be recalled that, according to Talmage, no reservation may be made respecting the *Book of Mormon* on the ground of incorrect translation, since this translation was effected through the gift and power of God.[19] This means, then, that Joseph Smith's translation differs from all other translations that have ever been made; it was inspired directly by God and is therefore completely errorless. This means, too, that the original manuscript of Smith's translation must be the authoritative one, since it embodies the translation as it is alleged to have come directly from God. No changes therefore may be tolerated in this original translation, since a single change would be sufficient to upset the theory that this was an errorless translation. The fact of the matter is, however, that a great many changes have been made in the *Book of Mormon* since the original edition of 1830 was published.[20] In comparing just the first chapter of this 1830 edition with the first chapter of the 1950 edition, I have noted nine changes, exclusive of punctuation. A number of these changes correct obvious grammatical errors. For example, "my father had read and saw" has been changed to "my father had read and seen"; "thy power, and goodness, and mercy is over all the inhabitants of the earth" has been changed to "thy power, and goodness, and mercy are over all the inhabitants of the earth"; "the tender mercies of the Lord is . . ." has been changed to "the tender mercies of the Lord are. . . ." Does the following sentence sound as though it has been inspired by God? "And when Moroni had said these words, he went forth among the people, waving the rent of his garment in the air, that all might see the writing which he had wrote upon the rent . . ." (Alma 46:19). The sentence has been changed to read: ". . . waving the rent part of his garment in the air, that all might see the writing which he had written upon the rent part. . . ." There have even been doctrinal corrections.

---

19 See above, p. 19.

20 Lamoni Call, in a book written in 1898, claimed that 2,038 corrections had been made in the *Book of Mormon* subsequent to the original edition (Arbaugh, *Revelation in Mormonism,* p. 50, n. 23). Arthur Budvarson, however, contends that by 1959 there had been over 3,000 changes (*The Book of Mormon Examined,* published by the Utah Christian Tract Society of La Mesa, Calif., 1959; p. 12).

An authentic copy of this original edition has been printed by the Deseret News Press in Salt Lake City: Wilford C. Wood, ed., *Joseph Smith Begins His Work,* Book of Mormon, 1830 First Edition (Deseret News Press, 1958). This volume contains no verse divisions.

On page 25 of the 1830 edition we read, "And the angel said unto me, behold the Lamb of God, yea, even the Eternal Father!" This has been corrected to read: "Behold the Lamb of God, yea, even the Son of the Eternal Father!" (I Nephi 11:21).

Does it seem likely that God would "inspire" a translation in which both grammatical and doctrinal corrections would have to be made? Mormons have no right to regard the grammatical errors as excusable on the ground of Smith's lack of formal education, for this entire translation is alleged to have been made "through the gift and power of God," and is said to be "in no sense the product of linguistic scholarship."[21] When there are occasional grammatical errors in our Bible translations — such as the notorious King James rendering of Matthew 16:15, "But whom say ye that I am?" — we have no difficulty in admitting that the translators, perhaps misled by the accusative case of the interrogative pronoun in the Greek, were in error. After all, no translator is inspired. But Mormons cannot admit even a single grammatical error in Smith's original translation.

Another difficulty we have with Smith's "translation" is the presence in it of at least 27,000 words from the King James Version of the Bible.[22] Does it seem likely that passages on the golden plates would be translated by divine inspiration in language precisely like that of the King James Bible?

We consider finally the testimony of Professor Charles Anthon, found in *Pearl of Great Price,* regarding the genuineness of the characters taken from the plates and the accuracy of the translation.[23] It will be recalled that when Anthon was shown the characters with their translation, he said, according to Smith's autobiography, that the translation was "correct, more so than any he had before seen translated from the Egyptian" (*Pearl of Great Price,* p. 55). However, in Mormon 9:34 we read, "But the Lord knoweth . . . that none other people knoweth our language; therefore he hath prepared means for the interpretation thereof." If the latter statement be correct, how could Professor Anthon know that the translation was correct? If, on the other hand, he could make a judgment as to the accuracy of the translation, it is not true that "none other people knoweth our language."

[21] Talmage, *Vitality of Mormonism.* p. 127.
[22] Budvarson, *op. cit.,* p. 22.
[23] See above, pp. 11-12.

Both Budvarson and Walter Martin reproduce the letter sent to Mr. E. D. Howe by Professor Anthon on February 17, 1834, in which the professor completely denies the truth of the statements attributed to him in the *Pearl of Great Price*.[24] Even apart from the existence of this letter, however, it will be obvious to any well-informed person that Professor Anthon could not have said what he is alleged to have said in *Pearl of Great Price*. For, according to this document, Anthon said, after he saw some characters supposedly copied from the golden plates, that these characters were: "Egyptian, Chaldaic, Assyriac, and Arabic" (p. 55). One would have expected a learned man, however, to designate which type of Egyptian script the characters represented: hieroglyphic, hieratic, or demotic. If we assume, now, that "Assyriac" stands for Assyrian, and that "Chaldaic" stands for some form of Aramaic, we may note that the professor is reported as saying that characters representing four different languages would provide a readable kind of writing! The matter is still further complicated when we observe that the cuneiform script used by the Assyrians, though it did employ syllabic signs and vowels, never became an alphabetic script,[25] that none of the three types of Egyptian writing were alphabetic scripts, and that both Aramaic and Arabic were written in alphabetic scripts. Does it seem likely that sense could be made out of characters from four different languages, two of which were written in alphabetic scripts, whereas the other two were not? To use an illustration, this would be like trying to write a sentence by putting letters from our own English alphabet next to some Hebrew consonants, some Japanese characters, and some Chinese characters! Is it not by this time clear that Professor Anthon, if he were any kind of scholar at all, could not possibly have said what the *Pearl of Great Price* reports him as having said? We may thus dismiss this supposedly learned testimony as completely valueless.

We conclude that there are so many improbabilities and absurdities in the story of the alleged "coming forth" of the *Book of Mormon* that it cannot possibly have been a genuine vehicle of divine revelation. In the words of a Mormon writer,

> This book [The *Book of Mormon*] must be either true or false. . . . If false, it is one of the most cunning, wicked, bold,

[24] Budvarson, *op. cit.,* pp. 39-40; Walter R. Martin, *The Maze of Mormonism* (Grand Rapids: Zondervan, 1962), pp. 42-44.
[25] Diringer, *op. cit.,* p. 43.

deep-laid impositions ever palmed upon the world, calculated
to deceive and ruin millions who would sincerely receive it as
the word of God, and will suppose themselves securely built
upon the rock of truth until they are plunged with their families
into hopeless despair.[26]

It is my earnest conviction that, in the light of the evidence presented in this appendix, the *Book of Mormon* is precisely what
Orson Pratt says it might be in the latter part of the above quotation.   It is, I believe, one of the most cunning and wicked impositions ever palmed upon the world.[27]

[26] Orson Pratt, *Divine Authenticity of the Book of Mormon;* quoted in
Budvarson, *op. cit.,* p. 7.

[27] An abbreviated version of this appendix has been prepared by the
author in the form of a 15-page tract entitled *The Bible and the Book
of Mormon.* This tract, which is addressed to Mormons and is intended
for use in evangelistic work with Mormons, can be obtained in quantities
from the Back to God Tract Committee, 2850 Kalamazoo Ave., Grand
Rapids, Mich., 49508.

Bibliography

PRIMARY SOURCES:

The Book of Mormon, Doctrine and Covenants, and *The Pearl of Great Price.* All three are published by the Church of Jesus Christ of Latter-day Saints at Salt Lake City, Utah.

(Note: Versions of *The Book of Mormon* and of *Doctrine and Covenants* published at Independence, Missouri, by the Reorganized Church of Jesus Christ of Latter Day Saints differ in some important respects from those published at Salt Lake City.)

Inspired Version of the Holy Scriptures. An Inspired Revision of the Authorized Version, by Joseph Smith, Jr. A New Corrected Edition. Independence: Herald Pub. House, 1955 (copyrighted in 1944).

(Note: This is the Bible version used by the Reorganized Mormon Church. Though Utah Mormons use the King James Version, they do accept all the changes made in the King James by Joseph Smith which have been incorporated into the "Inspired Version.")

Smith, Joseph Fielding, compiler. *Teachings of the Prophet Joseph Smith.* Salt Lake City: Deseret News Press, 1958. Excerpts from doctrinal sermons and writings of Joseph Smith.

Widtsoe, John A., compiler. *Discourses of Brigham Young.* Salt Lake City: Deseret Book Co., 1954. Selections gathered from the *Journal of Discourses,* arranged under 42 topics. 11-p. index.

BIOGRAPHICAL WORKS:

Biographies of Joseph Smith:

Brodie, Fawn M. *No Man Knows my History.* New York: Knopf, 1957.

Vander Valk, M. H. A. *De Profeet der Mormonen, Joseph Smith, Junior.* Kampen: Kok, 1921. Contains a 31-p. bibliography, with 1395 entries.

95

Biographies of Brigham Young:

Cannon, Frank J. and Knapp, George L. *Brigham Young and his Mormon Empire.* New York, 1913.

Gates, Susa Young. *The Life Story of Brigham Young.* London, 1930. Written by one of Young's daughters.

Werner, M. R. *Brigham Young.* New York: Harcourt, Brace, and Co., 1925.

WORKS DEALING PARTICULARLY WITH THE BOOK OF MORMON:

Budvarson, Arthur. *The Book of Mormon Examined.* La Mesa, Calif.: Utah Christian Tract Society, 1959. Now published by Zondervan under the title, *The Book of Mormon: True or False?* A critical examination of the Book of Mormon by a former Mormon.

Hunter, Milton R. *Archaeology and the Book of Mormon.* Vol. I. Salt Lake City: Deseret Book Co., 1956. An attempt to verify the truth of the Book of Mormon by means of archaeological evidence, chiefly from Central America.

Jonas, Larry W. *Mormon Claims Examined.* Grand Rapids: Baker, 1961. Contains correspondence from the Smithsonian Institution denying Mormon claims about the use of the Book of Mormon as a guide for archaeologists.

Kirkham, Francis W. *A New Witness for Christ in America.* 2 vols. Independence: Zion's Press, 1951. Pro-Mormon. Discusses the "divine origin of the Book of Mormon" and analyzes "the many attempts to prove the book man-made."

Reynolds, George. *A Complete Concordance to the Book of Mormon.* Salt Lake City: Deseret Book Co., 1957.

————. *The Story of the Book of Mormon.* Salt Lake City: Deseret Book Co., 1957. A "sacred" history, describing the events recorded in the Book of Mormon.

Roberts, Brigham H. *New Witnesses for God.* 3 vols. Salt Lake City: Deseret News Press, 1927. Cites many "external and internal evidences of the truth of the Book of Mormon."

Shook, Charles A. *The True Origin of the Book of Mormon.* Cincinnati: Standard Pub. Co., 1914. Anti-Mormon, by one who left the Mormon Church.

Sjodahl, J. M. *An Introduction to the Study of the Book of Mormon.* Salt Lake City: Deseret News Press, 1927.

Tanner, Jerald and Sandra. *3,913 Changes in the Book of Mormon.* Salt Lake City: Modern Microfilm Co., 1960. A photocopy of the original (1830) edition of the Book of Mormon, with all the subsequent changes marked in it.

Webb, R. C. *Joseph Smith as a Translator.* Salt Lake City: Deseret News Press, 1936. An attempt to show that Smith really did translate from Egyptian.

Wood, Wilford C. *Joseph Smith Begins his Work.* Salt Lake City: Deseret News Press, 1958. A photostatic copy of the first (1830) edition of the Book of Mormon. A comparison of this edition with the current one will reveal the many changes which have been made in the Book of Mormon.

WORKS DEALING PARTICULARLY WITH POLYGAMY:

Young, Ann Eliza. *Wife Number 19.* Hartford: Dustin, Gilman, 1879. An autobiography of Brigham Young's apostate wife.

Young, Kimball. *Isn't One Wife Enough?* New York: Holt, 1954. An exposition of plural marriage "in all its success and in all its sadness," by a grandson of Brigham Young.

WORKS DEALING PARTICULARLY WITH THE HISTORY OF MORMONISM:

Bancroft, Hubert H. *History of Utah.* San Francisco, 1890. Largely a history of the Mormons in Utah.

Beadle, John H. *Life in Utah;* or, The Mysteries and Crimes of Mormonism. Philadelphia, 1870.

Birney, Hoffman. *Zealots of Zion.* Philadelphia, 1931. A history of the early years of Mormonism.

Cannon, Frank J., and O'Higgins, Harvey J. *Under the Prophet in Utah:* The National Menace of a Political Priestcraft. Boston, 1911. A history of Mormonism in Utah from 1888 to 1911.

Hafen, Leroy R. *Handcarts to Zion.* Glendale: A. H. Clark, 1960. The story of a unique western migration (1856-1860).

————. *Journals of Forty-Niners.* Glendale: A. H. Clark, 1954. Salt Lake City to Los Angeles, with diaries.

Hinckley, Gordon B. *What of the Mormons?* Salt Lake City: Church of Jesus Christ of Latter-day Saints, 1954. Mostly historical; well illustrated.

Howe, Eber D. *Mormonism Unveiled.* Painesville, Ohio, 1834.

Howells, Rulon S. *The Mormon Story:* A Pictorial Account of Mormonism. Salt Lake City: Bookcraft, 1957 (10th ed., 1962). History, organization, practices, doctrines. Profusely illustrated.

Kelly, C., and Birney, H. *Holy Murder:* The Story of Porter Rockwell. New York, 1934. The biography of the executioner of early Mormonism.

Linn, W. A. *The Story of the Mormons* (from the date of their origin to the year 1901). New York: Macmillan, 1923 (copyrighted in 1902). Though old, one of the best historical studies.

Roberts, Brigham H. *A Comprehensive History of the Church of Jesus Christ of Latter-day Saints.* 6 vols. Salt Lake City: Deseret News Press, 1930.

Smith, Joseph, Jr. *The History of the Church of Jesus Christ of Latter-day Saints* (often referred to as the *Documentary History of the Church*). 6 vols. Salt Lake City: Deseret News, 1902-12.

Smith, Joseph Fielding. *Essentials in Church History.* 13th ed. Salt Lake City: Deseret News Press, 1953. An official history of the Mormon Church by the church historian.

West, Ray B., Jr. *Kingdom of the Saints.* The Story of Brigham Young and the Mormons. New York: Viking Press, 1957. A well-researched, appreciative history of Mormonism by a former Mormon.

(Note: the following is a history of Mormonism from the standpoint of the Reorganized Church:

Davis, Inez Smith. *The Story of the Church.* 6th ed.; 2nd revision. Independence: Herald Pub. House, 1959. Includes both the early history and that of the Reorganization.)

REFERENCE WORKS ON MORMONISM:

Brooks, Melvin R. *L. D. S. Reference Encyclopedia.* Salt Lake City: Bookcraft, 1960.

Jenson, Andrew. *Encyclopedic History of the Church of Jesus Christ of Latter-day Saints.* Salt Lake City: Deseret News Press, 1941. Gives historical details about various Mormon settlements and stakes.

DOCTRINAL STUDIES BY MORMON AUTHORS:

Bennion, Lowell L. *An Introduction to the Gospel.* Salt Lake City: Deseret Sunday School Union Board, 1955. A course of study for Sunday Schools.

————. *The Religion of the Latter-day Saints.* Salt Lake City: Latter-day Saints' Department of Education, 1940. A guide to Mormon doctrines for college students.

Berrett, Wm. E. *Teachings of the Doctrine and Covenants.* Salt Lake City, 1954. A Sunday School Manual.

Hunter, Milton R. *The Gospel Through the Ages.* Salt Lake City: Deseret Book Co., 1958 (copyrighted in 1945). A doctrinal study intended especially for Mormon missionaries.

McConkie, Bruce R. *Mormon Doctrine.* Salt Lake City: Bookcraft, 1958. A detailed exposition of Mormon doctrine in encyclopedic form.

Richards, LeGrand. *A Marvelous Work and a Wonder.* Salt Lake City: Deseret Book Co., 1950. An exposition of Mormon doctrines particularly intended for missionaries.

Smith, Hyrum M., and Sjodahl, Janne M. *Doctrine and Covenants Commentary.* Rev. ed. Salt Lake City: Deseret, 1960 (copyrighted in 1951). Historical and explanatory notes.

Smith, Joseph F. *Gospel Doctrine.* 12th ed. Salt Lake City: Deseret News Press, 1961 (copyrighted 1939). Selections from the sermons and writings of Joseph F. Smith (1838-1918), the 6th president of the Mormon Church and the father of Joseph Fielding Smith.

Smith, Joseph Fielding. *Answers to Gospel Questions.* 3 vols. Salt Lake City: Deseret Book Co., 1958. A series of answers to questions pertaining to Scripture, doctrine, and history, submitted over a period of years, and answered in the Mormon periodical, *The Improvement Era.*

————. *Doctrines of Salvation.* 3 vols. Salt Lake City: Bookcraft, 1960 (copyrighted 1954-56). Compiled from the sermons and writings of Joseph Fielding Smith, by Bruce R. McConkie. The most complete and most recent discussion of Mormon doctrine presently available.

Talmage, James E. *A Study of the Articles of Faith.* 36th ed. Salt Lake City: Church of Jesus Christ of Latter-day Saints, 1957 (first published in 1899). An exposition of the Mormon Articles of Faith. A standard source-book for Mormon doctrines.

————. *The Vitality of Mormonism.* Boston: R. G. Badger, 1919. Brief essays on distinctive Mormon doctrines.

Widtsoe, John A. *Evidences and Reconciliations.* Arranged by G. H. Durham. 3 vols. in 1. Salt Lake City: Bookcraft, 1960. A series of answers to questions, involving doctrine, science, history, ethics, and church rules, submitted to the author over a period of years.

————. *A Rational Theology.* 6th ed. Salt Lake City: Deseret Book Co., 1952 (copyrighted in 1915). An exposition of Mormon theology, somewhat philosophically oriented.

(Note: The following volume is a study of the differences in doctrine and practice between the Reorganized Church and the Utah Church:

Ralston, Russell F. *Fundamental Differences Between the Reorganized Church and the Church in Utah.* Independence: Herald Pub. House, 1960. 244 pp.)

GENERAL WORKS:

BOOKS:

Arbaugh, George B. *Gods, Sex, and Saints*: The Mormon Story. Rock Island: Augustana Press, 1957. Deals with polytheism, other Mormon doctrines, and the approach to Mormons.

————. *Revelation in Mormonism.* Chicago: University of Chicago Press, 1932. A doctoral dissertation dealing with the Mormon conception of divine revelation.

Bennett, Wallace F. *Why I am a Mormon.* New York: T. Nelson, 1958.

Ericksen, Ephraim E. *The Psychological and Ethical Aspects of Mormon Group Life.* Chicago: University of Chicago Press, 1922.

Kinney, Bruce. *Mormonism: The Islam of America*. Rev. and enlarged ed. New York: Revell, 1912. The author was formerly
superintendent of Baptist missions in Utah.
La Rue, Wm. E. *The Foundations of Mormonism*. New York:
Revell, 1919.
Martin, Walter R. *The Maze of Mormonism*. Grand Rapids: Zon-
dervan, 1962. History, doctrines, public relations. Has chapter on
how to meet Mormon missionaries.
McNiff, W. J. *Heaven on Earth*: A Planned Mormon Society. Ox-
ford, Ohio: Mississippi Valley Press, 1940. A study of Mormon
culture.
O'Dea, Thomas F. *The Mormons*. Chicago: University of Chicago
Press, 1957. Based partly on a Harvard dissertation. Includes
historical, psychological, and sociological insights.
Sheldon, Henry C. *A Fourfold Test of Mormonism*. New York:
Abingdon Press, 1914.
Snowden, James H. *The Truth about Mormonism*. New York:
George H. Doran, 1926. A study of the history, doctrines, and
practices of Mormonism.
Tanner, Jerald and Sandra. *Archaeology and the Book of Mormon*.
Salt Lake City: Modern Microfilm Co., n. d. Shows that archaeological
findings on the American continents do not support the Book of
Mormon.
————. *The Case Against Mormonism*. 3 vols. Salt Lake City:
Modern Microfilm Co., 1967-71. Written by former Mormons, this
work presents a devastating case against the divine authority of Mor-
mon religious documents. Vol. I deals with Joseph's first vision,
changes in Mormon revelations and documents, suppression of the
records, and the like. Vol. II deals with the witnesses to the Book of
Mormon, the golden plates, and parallels between the Book of Mor-
mon and other documents. Vol. III deals with the Book of Abraham,
the plurality of gods, the Adam-God doctrine, and false prophecies of
Joseph Smith and Brigham Young.
————. *The Mormon Kingdom*. 2 vols. Salt Lake City: Modern
Microfilm Co., 1969-71. Discusses the temple ceremony, blood atone-
ment, baptism for the dead, and the relationship between Mormonism
and Masonry.
————. *Mormonism — Shadow or Reality*. Enlarged ed. Salt Lake
City: Modern Microfilm Co., 1972. A thoroughly documented polemic
against Mormonism. The Tanners' most comprehensive volume.
Turner, Wallace. *The Mormon Establishment*. Boston: Houghton
Mifflin, 1966. An account of present-day Mormonism.
Van Dellen, I. *Het Mormonisme*. Kampen: Kok, 1911. A study of
Mormonism by a Christian Reformed minister.
Vander Valk, M. H. A. *De Mormonen: Hun Profeet, Leer, en Leven*.
Kampen: Kok, 1924. A popular study by the author of *De
Profeet der Mormonen* (see above).

Walters, Wesley P. *New Light on Mormon Origins.* La Mesa, Calif.: Utah Christian Tract Society, 1967. Disproves Joseph Smith's claim that a religious revival occurring in Palmyra, New York, in 1820 led to the beginnings of Mormonism.

Whalen, Wm. J. *The Latter-day Saints in the Modern Day World.* N.Y.: John Day Co., 1964. An account of contemporary Mormonism by a Roman Catholic layman.

PAMPHLETS:

(Note: Pastors and missionaries desiring inexpensive booklets for distribution to parishioners and inquirers are referred to the following list.)

Anderson, Einar. *Mormonism* (A Personal Testimony). Chicago: Moody Press, 1956. 32 pp.

Anderson, Rodger I. *The Bible and Mormonism.* Faith, Prayer, and Tract League; Grand Rapids, Mich. 49504. 24 pp.

Fraser, Gordon H. *Is Mormonism Christian?* An Examination of Mormon Doctrine as Compared with Orthodox Christianity. Chicago: Moody Press, 1957. 122 pp. An excellent brief survey.

Hoekema, Anthony A. *The Bible and the Book of Mormon.* Back to God Tract Committee, 2850 Kalamazoo Ave., Grand Rapids, Mich. 49508. 15 pp.

Martin, Walter R. *Mormonism.* Grand Rapids: Zondervan, 1957. 32 pp.

Nutting, John D. *Mormonism Today and its Remedy.* Cleveland: Utah Gospel Mission, 1927. 20 pp. Brief account of doctrines, practices, and history.

Smith, John L. *Has Mormonism Changed?* Clearfield, Utah: Utah Evangel Press, 1959. 59 pp. Discusses missionary work among Mormons, history, and doctrines.

————. *Hope or Despair.* Clearfield, Utah: Utah Evangel Press, 1959. 35 pp. Brief criticism of Mormon doctrines, including 10 photostatic reprints, some from the *Journal of Discourses.*

Talbot, Louis T. *What's Wrong with Mormonism?* Findlay, Ohio: Dunham Pub. Co., 1957. 48 pp.

(Note: Some of the above pamphlets can be obtained from Religion Analysis Service, 902 Hennepin Ave., Minneapolis 3, Minn.)